Local Administration
in West Africa

by the same author

CORRUPTION IN DEVELOPING COUNTRIES
(*with Edgar Simpkins*)

EAST AFRICAN CITIZEN (O.U.P.)

GUGGISBERG: A Biography of Sir Gordon Guggisberg
(O.U.P.)

Local Administration in West Africa

BY

RONALD WRAITH C.B.E.

*Fellow of the Institute of Local
Government Studies, University
of Birmingham*

AFRICANA PUBLISHING CORPORATION
NEW YORK

Published in the United States of America 1972
by Africana Publishing Corporation
101 Fifth Avenue
New York, N.Y. 10003

FIRST PUBLISHED AS *Local Government in West Africa* 1964

SECOND EDITION 1972

This book is copyright under the Berne Convention. All rights are reserved. Apart from any fair dealing for the purpose of private study, research, criticism or review, as permitted under the Copyright Act, 1956 no part of this publication may be reproduced, stored in a retrieval system, or transmitted, in any form or by any means, electronic, electrical, chemical, mechanical, optical, photocopying, recording or otherwise, without the prior permission of the copyright owner. Enquiries should be addressed to the publishers.

ISBN 0 8419 0123 6

© *George Allen & Unwin Ltd*, 1964, 1972
Library of Congress Catalog
Card No. 72-76471

PRINTED IN GREAT BRITAIN

PREFACE

THIS book is a revision of *Local Government in West Africa*, which was published in 1964. The change in title reflects changes in the reality, as it is hoped the book will make clear.

The first three chapters of Part I are new. The remaining ones are a revision of the previous book; they deal with aspects of local government which do not change, but when any reference is made to a particular situation in West Africa it is now written in the past tense, as it refers to the 1960s, before the civil war in Nigeria and the change of the régime in Ghana. These references have some historical interest and are a help in understanding the present position.

Part II presents a sketch of the situation as it was in the early part of 1971. It is unfortunate that the author had no alternative but to bring himself up-to-date at that particular time, as a number of important changes were pending; for example, a new Act of Parliament in Ghana, fundamental changes in the South-Eastern and East Central States of Nigeria and Reports of Commissions in Sierra Leone and the State of Lagos. However, all these changes will take some years to show their effects, and although a visit to West Africa even six months later would have been more profitable in the collection of detailed material it is hoped that enough has been included to indicate the general direction in which local government is moving.

To avoid awkward repetition the phrase 'West Africa' is used throughout to mean anglophone West Africa.

ACKNOWLEDGEMENT

The revision of the book was made possible by the generosity of the Institute of Local Government Studies of the University of Birmingham, which enabled the author to re-visit West Africa in January/February 1971.

CONTENTS

PART I

Preface	7
1. *Decentralization*	13
2. *The Ecology of Local Government*	27
3. *The Function of Local Government*	41
4. *Local Authorities*	54
Their Constitutional Basis	
Their Relationship with each other	
Their Relationship with the Central Government	
5. *People in Local Government*	76
The Elected Councillors	
The Full-time Staff	
6. *Party Politics in Local Government*	110
7. *The Revenue of Local Authorities*	119

PART II

8. *The Cities of West Africa*	139
9. *Sierra Leone*	152
10. *Ghana*	166
11. *Nigeria*	179
The East	
The West	
The North	
12. *Conclusion*	216
Index	235

PART I

CHAPTER 1

Decentralization

'This term refers to the transfer of authority on a geographic basis, whether by *deconcentration* (i.e. delegation) of authority to field units of the same department or level of government, or by *devolution* of authority to local government units or special statutory bodies. This meaning, although differing from that of the French term *décentralisation*, is one given to the term in a number of countries and is useful for the purpose of this report.'

> United Nations, *Decentralisation for National and Local Development* (New York 1965), pp. 88–9.

THIS definition need not be taken literally, but it is a useful introduction to our subject because it puts 'local government' into its wider context as one of several aspects of public administration. Translated into visual form it would look something like this:

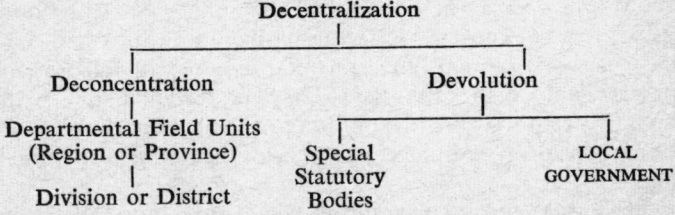

In these terms the old British colonial administration was a form of 'deconcentration'. A country was divided into large units which were usually called 'provinces', and at the head of the provincial administration was a man variously called a Chief Commissioner or Resident. He was the chief administrator, but alongside him were provincial departmental heads—the Provincial Engineer, Medical Officer of Health, Education Officer, Agricultural Officer and others. They had offices, equipment and staff at the provincial headquarters and were the effective agency in the province for providing public works, clinics, schools, agricultural modernization and so forth. The provinces were sub-divided into areas known as divisions in Nigeria and districts in Ghana and Sierra Leone. Their administrative head was called either a District Officer or District Commissioner, and his work was both administrative and judicial. So far as his administrative duties were concerned he was supposed to be *primus inter pares* with the professional and technical officers who were working in his division, and to seek their help or co-ordinate their activities. Whether the central government departments had field staff at the divisional as well as provincial level varied a good deal with circumstances. But administrative, professional and technical staff alike took their orders from above—from the Chief Secretary in the one case and from the Heads of Departments on the other, and they were not accountable to the people among whom they worked.

True, at the divisional or district level there was a rudimentary form of local government known as the 'native authority', from which such local government as exists in West Africa today has developed. Beginning as little more than local customary courts the native authorities had, by the end of colonial government, acquired much wider powers and responsibilities. They represented the first tentative step towards 'devolution'; in their more developed form—'local government'—they are the subject of this book.

The other form of devolution which the United Nations definition identifies is that which is exercised through 'special statutory bodies'. These are in effect the governing bodies of nationalized industries or public utilities over which a government must exercise ultimate control, since they are vital to the public interest, but which must be run commercially and (in the long term at any rate) show a financial surplus. Great social services such as health and education do not have to think in terms of expenditure and income; money income, such as fees etc., is insignificant, and the entry on the credit side of the account is simply the improved health and intelligence of the populace in the foreseeable future. But an electricity undertaking or an airline, or docks and harbours, must be run like commercial enterprises and pay their way—and there is a universal belief that the bureaucracy of civil service departments, excellent though it may be in controlling expenditure, preventing waste and safeguarding the taxpayers' money, is unsuitable for activities which demand business judgment and commercial risk. Accordingly there have come into being great numbers of public boards and corporations, which are, so to speak, the offspring of a marriage between government departments and private commercial enterprise. That is to say, a minister has ultimate responsibility for them and is accountable to Government and Parliament for their success or failure. Normally, however, he is only responsible for broad policy and providing them with funds; he delegates the day-to-day running to a board or corporation, whose members are nominated by himself, which has full freedom in technical, commercial and financial management, uninhibited by political or civil service control. This is the theory and the ideal. In practice it is a difficult relationship either to define exactly or to maintain, and there have been many failings, through the inability of political parties to leave them alone, or of ministers to resist pressures to interfere in their management.

The broad principles of the matter, however, are clear, i.e. there is a distinction between overall policy and day-to-day management. Accordingly the minister *devolves* his responsibilities on to a quasi-independent body, which is also representative, for although he appoints them in his full discretion he is bound by statute to take account of all the principal interests, such as trade unions, the general public as consumers, and employers or management.

Their ramifications, on the other hand, are immensely complicated. Such boards or corporations may control an enterprise which is a natural monopoly, and which, in the public interest, ought not to be exploited for individual enrichment, e.g. the coal industry, a supply of electricity or water, the provision of an airline or broadcasting service, the running of a country's principal port. All these are activities which have in the past and in other parts of the world been run by competitive private enterprise—as indeed some of them are today—but in which there has been a general tendency towards public control in the interests of both efficiency and equity. To these, which are common throughout the developed world, may be added a number which are especially characteristic of the poorer countries, e.g. housing corporations, in situations where there is not enough private capital accumulation to meet the demand for houses; general development corporations to prime the pump, and also in situations where private capital and enterprise is insufficient to get new enterprises going; and finance corporations to advance loans to the farmers or entrepreneurs. The governments of the new West African countries have in fact unwisely allowed such boards to proliferate in areas which were either inappropriate or premature, often with disastrous losses.

Seen at their best, however, and in their legitimate sphere, they are one of the two main kinds of devolution in public administration, and their importance is still growing in many countries of the world, often unobtrusively and without the general public realizing how much of their life has come to be governed by them. In Britain today the average citizen's life is probably just as much affected by the activities of non-elected boards as by those of elected local authorities—they operate in such diverse fields as hospitals; electricity, gas, water; public assistance; the administration of new towns; transportation. For it is important to remember that these controlling bodies are not elected, except in the very indirect sense that the minister who appoints them is himself an elected Member of Parliament. But no one is elected to a Hospital Board, in the sense in which they are elected to a Town Council.

We have, then, two main streams—deconcentration and devolution, the second of which is fed by two tributaries of equal importance—special statutory bodies and local authorities. The rest of this book will be largely concerned with the latter; but not wholly, since although blackboard diagrams are neat and tidy, real life is muddled and illogical, and one cannot always distinguish between the various aspects of public administration as clearly on the ground as one can from the top of an ivory tower.

At this point it is necessary to digress, and to say that the expression 'local government' is by no means an exact one, but can mean different things in different parts of the world. Indeed, as we shall see in the next chapter, it is so much a product of a particular local environment that there are almost as many different kinds of local government as there are countries or nations. Nevertheless, a broad classification of the major types can be helpful, and it has been supplied by Professor Harold F. Alderfer.[1] According to him there are four basic patterns of local government in the world today—the French, the Anglo-Saxon,[2] the Communist and the traditional.

In the French system, which is probably the most widespread of them all, local government may properly be regarded as the local arm of the central government. Local councils (*conseils municipals*) have indeed important powers and duties, exercised through their principal officer

---

[1] *Local Government in Developing Countries*, McGraw-Hill, New York 1964, pp. 1–16.
[2] Professor Alderfer uses the word 'English', but the broad category he describes includes, for example, Western Germany, Scandinavia, North America and Australasia.

the Mayor; but their proceedings are subject to the direction, approval or veto of a civil servant (the *Préfect*) who represents the Government of France in its every aspect. The *Préfects* represent a corps of highly-trained, extremely able local governors, and there is a rough parallel to be drawn between the *Préfect* and the old colonial Resident or Commissioner on the one hand, and the *conseil municipal* and the old native authority on the other; in other words the British administrators of colonial days were operating a system of local government which more resembled that of France than of Britain.

The characteristic of the Anglo-Saxon type of local government, on the other hand, is local autonomy, exercised through locally elected councils. This can never be absolute, for there can only be one sovereign authority in a state, and moreover a government today has a duty to ensure that the services which local councils provide are reasonably efficient and reasonably uniform throughout the country, and must consequently exercise control. The degree of autonomy will naturally vary from one country to another, and it may vary, as in Britain, between one kind of service and another. But always there will be the concept of a division of labour, or a partnership, between central government and an elected local authority, in which the government respects some degree of independence in the local body.

The characteristic of Communist local government is that it is part of a complex of governmental agencies whose purpose is socialistic planning for the economic development of the community, a process in which the Party exercises firm direction and leadership. The concept of 'democratic centralism' on which it is based has had considerable appeal in West Africa, partly because in some of its aspects it reflects traditional African political practice, and partly because of the impressive material achievements of Soviet Communism; but West Africa is stony soil for other aspects of Communism and it has not been a deep influence in local government.

Professor Alderfer's final classification is somewhat unsatisfactory, as he himself admits. Broadly he means 'non-western', but 'western' influences are now so far-reaching that little remains unaffected by them, even in the villages of the 'third world'. He is referring, however, to the many traditional types of local government in the pre-literate and undeveloped world which are conveniently summed-up in the word 'tribal', and which are associated with, for example, a chief or traditional leader, a council of elders, the extended family or clan, or with ancient custom or ritual.

These four categories throw some light on the subject and are convenient for the kind of exposition which this book attempts. They are not, however, clear-cut or mutually exclusive, for they may influence each other and compromises may exist between them. For example, local autonomy in Britain is modified by an increasing amount of central control, while prefectorial government in France is increasingly subject to the democratic influence of the *conseils municipals*. There are other variations on the theme. In the United States, for example, a dozen different patterns of local government may be found, varying from east to west of the continent and from rural to urban areas. The government of big cities is carried on variously by elected Boards of Commissioners, who after election become administrators in their own right, by 'political bosses' who exercise great personal authority, or by 'city managers', who are professional administrators hired by the elected city councils to run the affairs of the city with a high degree of independence. The last variation is particularly interesting, as it brings to local government the approach of 'big business'; that is to say the city manager and the city council have some resemblance to the managing director and the board of directors of a large firm.

But perhaps West Africa itself provides the best example of 'cross-fertilization' between different categories. In Ghana, for example, the French and Anglo-Saxon concepts existed side by side in colonial days, the Anglo-Saxon making slight but on the whole insignificant inroads on the French; with independence the Government of Ghana first leant more heavily on English tradition and practice, but later, at the height of Nkrumah's power, acquired strong overtones of 'democratic centralism'. At the time of writing it is attempting a new form of 'local administration' which again combines French and Anglo-Saxon influences, but in different proportions from the colonial era.[3] But throughout the twentieth century each of these foreign influences, corresponding to Alderfer's first three categories, has in turn been influenced by the fourth category—the traditional. The influence of the Gold Coast and Ghanaian chiefs has fluctuated from greater power than tradition accorded them under British indirect rule to near humiliation under Nkrumah; but it was never extinguished, and now, at the village level, the chiefs' place on local government has been written into the Constitution. In a mere twenty-five years, therefore, Ghana may be said to have touched Professor Alderfer's analysis at every point.

But to return to our original theme, public administration in all countries, whether they are industrialized and wealthy or pre-industrial and poor, contains elements of both deconcentration and devolution. It is not a question of one or the other, but of the balance between them. In countries in the French or Communist traditions of government it is self-evident that decentralization takes the form of deconcentration[4]—put more simply there is a hierarchical structure or chain of command. In the Anglo-Saxon countries, and in anglophone West Africa, which is still in the formative stage in local government, there is more flexibility and it is possible to attempt a generalization, namely that as countries 'develop', i.e. as their education and standards of living rise, decentralization tends to take

[3] The point is discussed further on pp. 166–78.
[4] It is interesting that the United Nations definition which we have used is unacceptable to the French, to whom the two words are indistinguishable.

the form of devolution to local authorities, while in the undeveloped countries it takes the form of deconcentration. Thus local authorities have great power in Britain, West Germany, Scandinavia, the Low Countries and the United States; but very little power in Nigeria, Ghana and Sierra Leone.

No doubt it is part of a natural process that as education and prosperity become more widespread people demand, and are capable of exercising, an increasing share of responsibility in administering local affairs, and that there is a likelihood that the balance changes in response to progress. This, however, is an academic question that need not detain us here. Much more to the point is the fact—to which we must return from time to time—that the characteristic problem of the developing countries of West Africa is that they are trying to follow the two paths of deconcentration and devolution without the material resources of manpower, equipment and finance to follow either successfully. Their basic problem is to deploy scarce resources to the best advantage, and this dual pursuit is wasteful of such resources as they possess.

Moreover, because of the overall shortage of resources, there is not enough work to occupy the energies both of a field administration of the central government and of effective local government. This is a dilemma peculiar to those former British dependencies where during colonial days the French or deconcentrated system of administration was practised by the British, but where in the closing days of colonial rule attempts were made to erect the British apparatus of devolution, as exemplified especially by a British type of local government.

Such was the importance that was attached to local government at this time that laws were rushed on to the statute book, and local councils were created with comprehensive powers on paper but with little in the way of human or material resources to exercise them. Meanwhile the field administration of government departments continued unchanged, unaffected by these experiments in devolution—

so that local authorities were in reality in competition with the provincial and district officials of government departments, a competition in which they were of course seriously handicapped.

Quite apart from the question of whether there is likely to be a trend from deconcentration towards devolution as a country develops, it should be noticed that local administration as it actually exists in many parts of Africa is already a mixture of the two, and that the patterns of relationship are so varied that it is sometimes difficult to disentagle local from central government. It is worth looking at a few of them.

First it is important to reiterate what has already been said, that in no circumstances can local government be *independent*. This may seem an obvious point, but misunderstanding about it has done a great deal of harm in Africa in the past. It is well known that administrative boundaries tend to follow tribal or ethnic boundaries, and talk about local *self*-government—a misleading and exaggerated phrase—has given rise to suspicion that what local government means is tribal independence and consequent national disunity. Throughout Africa the paramount need of the new states is to create national unity, and if local government becomes a divisive influence it would be better to do without it and to have an openly centralized form of administration. In Anglophone West Africa, however, there is enough understanding of local government, from 20 years of rather painful experience, to know that self-government and independence are not supposed to be among its attributes. There is a good deal more doubt as to the *degree* of independence which local authorities can properly expect, and experience of this, throughout the whole of Anglophone Africa, is very varied.

In the first place there is the Government Agent, by whatever name he may now be known. He is the direct descendant of the old DO or DC, and although as an African working among his own people he does not always have the fortuitious prestige of his European predecessor he is nevertheless an all-purpose officer of considerable standing. In colonial days the British DO had even greater standing; he was the representative of the ruling power; he possessed magisterial as well as administrative functions; and he ranked above his own expatriate colleagues in the professional and technical services. The DO today has been stripped of a good deal of this authority and mystique and generally speaking, although he is still theoretically first among equals he is in practice more concerned with local government than with anything else and is often in reality the local representative of the Ministry of Local Government. He is, moreover, much more susceptible to political pressures, both local and national, than his expatriate predecessor, and may, in different degrees in different countries, have to be acceptable to, if not openly allied with, the ruling political party.

This is a situation which has no parallel in local government in any country in the Anglo-Saxon tradition, where there is no *all-purpose* local representative of the central government, though there may be regional or provincial representatives of particular departments, and where public servants are, though admittedly in varying degrees, more insulated from political parties. Accordingly his mere presence places local government under a direct tutelage of a kind which can often cause difficulty or friction. In Uganda, to take an extreme example, the basic local government unit is very large, corresponding to a kingdom or province or—what is more to the point—the administrative area of the 'Government Agent'; in these circumstances the relationship between the two officers is somewhat difficult to define.

But leaving aside the actual presence of a local officer of central government—a 'sub-prefect' in French terms—there are a number of shades of relationship between local and central government.

First, there is the position of local government staff. Towards the end of the colonial era, when 'native administration' was first giving way to 'local government', it was an assumption, derived from British models, that the new local authorities would employ their own staff, and be free to appoint men of their own choice to every job from that of treasurer to office cleaner, and to dismiss them at their pleasure. As time went by this was found to be impracticable and has been greatly modified, so that there have come into being a variety of schemes for 'unified' or 'centralized' local government services which gave governments varying degrees of control over local government staff. These matters are discussed fully in chapter 5, and the only point of introducing them here is that they very aptly illustrate the difficulty of keeping 'deconcentration' (the civil service) and 'devolution' (locally employed staffs) in water-tight compartments.

The point is again illustrated by various kinds of 'secondment' (also discussed in chapter 5) whereby civil servants temporarily become chief officers in local authorities, serving two masters—the head of their substantive department and the council to whose service they are appointed. A different but related kind of link between the centre and the circumference has sometimes been seen in African states in the practice whereby the central government field staff—engineers, agriculturalists, educationists and so on—sit as *ex officio* members, though usually without voting rights, on local councils. This was widely practised at one stage in the development of local government in Kenya, at the District Council level, and had a number of advantages. It gave the departmental officers an opportunity of explaining government policies which might not otherwise have been understood by most ordinary people and it meant that in coming to decisions about any kind of new development technical advice was available to keep the decisions of the local council in line with practical realities. This practice has now been established, at any rate at the regional level, in the new Ghana Local Administration Act of 1971.

Finally, we have already said that administration in any

country in the world is a mixture of deconcentration and devolution, and that what really matters is the balance between them. The point of balance, however, can determine whether we are basically considering field administration by the central government, operating through local authorities as a kind of agency, or quasi-autonomous local government over which the central government exercises no more control than is necessary in the national interest. There are not many examples of the latter in the whole of Anglophone Africa. In former days some of the biggest cities approached this definition, with their elected councils and well-defined responsibilities, principally in the field of public health. Some ancient kingdoms, such as Buganda or Ashanti, also used to have considerable freedom of action in 'modern' as well as traditional affairs as did the well-established local administrations of the Muslim emirates. But so far as municipal government is concerned, although their responsibilities remain in the established realms of sanitation, minor works and primary education many modern developments such as town planning, slum clearance and housing, sewerage, drainage and other municipal public utilities have by-passed them and are centrally administered; while the administration of kingdoms and emirates is slowly but inexorably being brought in accord with universal bureaucratic patterns.

As to the smaller units—the district or division—their freedom of action was never very spacious. They have always been under a necessary but frustrating obligation to submit their budgets and many of their decisions for ratification by higher authority, and currently they are under the fairly strict tutelage of administrative officers; so much so that it is not easy to fit them into the formal pattern of the United Nations chart. They are presently neither one thing nor the other.

What is important to remember is that the pendulum swings, and that during times of political and indeed military crisis it is bound to swing rather violently. Generally speaking there has been a swing in government in West Africa from decentralization to centralization, and within the decentralized zone from devolution to deconcentration. This may be temporary. As the book will try to show, local government in Sierra Leone, Ghana and Nigeria is at the time of writing in a kind of limbo. The overthrow of the Nkrumah régime in Ghana and the civil war in Nigeria brought to an end the rather fumbling attempts of the 1950s and 1960s to establish 'efficient and representative local government' in a modern and unduly British form; for some years the former councils were replaced by administrators or committees of management; new thinking has now resulted in fresh legislation, but this will take some years to bear fruit and it cannot reasonably be assessed at the moment.

The United Nations definition at the head of this chapter was written as a guide to the analysis of public administration in normal, settled times. Its usefulness is somewhat limited by the suspension of normal political activity and the centralizing tendencies of military rule, but it has sufficient validity even in abnormal times to put local government in perspective in the total picture of public administration.

CHAPTER 2

The Ecology of Local Government

> *Ecology*: Branch of biology dealing with living organisms' habits, modes of life and relations to their surroundings (Oxford Dictionary).

It is useful to think of the formative stages of local government in these terms, for they suggest two things which need constantly to be borne in mind—first, that local government is an 'organism', something that cannot be contained for ever—or even for very long—in a particular set of statutes, rules and regulations, but which is constantly adapting itself to new circumstances; and secondly that it is related to 'habits, modes of life and surroundings'. It follows that it will differ from one country to another, or even within one country; for example it will be different in Scotland from England, in northern Nigeria from southeastern Nigeria, in Ghana from Sierra Leone. The factors which bring about these differences, and help to determine different patterns and purposes for local government, are very complex, and include the historical, the geographical, the sociological, the political and the economic.

HISTORY is so important that it is no exaggeration to say that local government in any country can only be understood in terms of its history. There can be no better example of this than the fundamental difference between France and Britain, two countries with centuries of close dealing and separated only by a few miles of water.

The ground for the present-day system of local government in France was prepared by the French Revolution, which swept away much that had existed under the previous Bourbon monarchies and paved the way for Napoleon, in 1800, to introduce a system characterized, in the words of Professor Alderfer, by 'centralization, chain of command, hierarchical structure, executive domination and legislative subordination'. It has been a good deal modified since Napoleon's day. The basic unit of local government, the *commune*, now has an elected council which elects its own *maire*, who is the chief executive official. But the responsibilities of the council are narrow and its work is subject to direction and review by the *sous-préfect* and the *préfect*, agents of the Ministry of the Interior; while the *maire*, once chosen by the people, becomes himself an executive agent of the Government and must reconcile his duty to the council which elected him with his higher duty to the prefecture. Accordingly, as we said on p. 17, local government is essentially the local arm of central government.

Britain never had a revolution, but evolved slowly and on the whole peacefully, always tending to carry something from the past with her as changes in government and administration took place. Moreover, in many matters which are considered important today local government preceded central government, and this historical fact largely accounts for the unusually prominent part which it plays, relative to the central government, in the administration of the country. Literally speaking, government in some of the ancient towns or boroughs preceded the existence of national government itself, but something of the same sort could be said of most of Africa until very recent times, and it is of no particular significance. What is more important is that in the nineteenth century, when modern social problems were taking shape, the power and the means to solve them were given to locally elected bodies rather than to local agents of the central government. To some extent Britain was caught unawares by these problems and solved them in the most convenient and pragmatic way, but in a way which was to set the pattern of administration in the twentieth century. It has to be remembered that Britain was the pioneer country in two vital matters—the agricultural revolution which brought about the enclosure of the land and the dispossession of the peasant; and the industrial revolution which created vast, unplanned, insanitary towns. These two 'revolutions' were as traumatic in their way as political or military revolution, for they created unprecedented social problems, especially of destitution and disease.

The central government itself had no machinery for tackling these problems. In accordance with the thinking of the times it stood aloof from what we now call social problems and its few departments were concerned with trade, foreign affairs, defence, internal law and order and questions of a similar kind. 'Local government', as it then existed, was equally incapable of solving them. Outside the boroughs (which were in any case concerned with local trade and prosperity and were extremely corrupt) local government meant the 'justices of the peace', whose main purpose was judicial and whose administrative functions were rudimentary. Moreover, the justices were for the most part essentially men of the land—farmers and rural aristocracy—who neither sympathized with nor were capable of understanding the new social problems, which were essentially urban and industrial.

But the problems, as is the habit with such problems, did not go away; someone had to try to solve them, and the policy of nineteenth-century governments was to give responsibility to locally elected bodies with the power to levy a local rate. One such body after another was created —to deal with poverty, with basic necessities in the streets, with sanitation and public health, and later with public education. Towards the century's end they coalesced into the system which still exists, largely unchanged, at the time of writing. To follow these developments in detail would be beyond the scope of this book; the immediate point is that a particular set of historical circumstances, peculiar to this one country, helped to cast local government in a particular mould.

It is ironical that British African colonies should have adopted a form of local government which grew from these historical circumstances, because their own history, in these respects, was so different. When comparable 'modern' problems began to arise in the twentieth century Government was paternal and all-powerful and its local agents, the district commissioners, were supposed to solve every problem that came along. State control, which would have been regarded in Britain at that time as socialist and therefore unacceptable, was accepted in colonial government as normal. To get a true British-African comparison it is therefore necessary to stand history on its head. The result, in Africa, of superimposing the British kind of local government on what already existed was simply too much government; there was not enough for everyone to do, especially with the limited resources available, so that having created local government it was necessary to invent a purpose for it. In fact, the real purpose, in the minds of the British, had been political education, as a preparation for self-government, and in the minds of the African politicians the diminution of the power of the chiefs.

The colonial era is, of course, a part of African history, and its influence will always be important. It is, however, only an era, of little more than half a century, and before local government in Africa can assume any form that could be called characteristic it must take account of what happened before and since this era. In actual fact British colonial rule did not impose much uniformity in local administration; indeed the doctrine of indirect rule—of governing through indigenous institutions and authorities—was itself a denial of uniformity, since none existed in the indigenous authorities. Thus the administration of a Muslim 'emirate', an Ibo 'town' (i.e. group of villages) and a Yoruba 'kingdom' had almost nothing in common with each other. It is true that experience had taught the British to look for a natural ruler or chief, and they were disposed to invent one if they could not find him. Thus in parts of the eastern provinces of Nigeria, where natural rulers had not existed, they delegated authority to 'warrant chiefs' who were convenient spokesmen—even 'stooges'—of Government, but were not regarded by the local people as anything but government agents. On the whole, however, local administration under the British followed the grain of history in as far as that history was known and understood. It was only after 1947, when a conscious effort was made to replace traditional native administration by modern local government, that uniformity began—the uniformity that arose from legislation adapted first by the Eastern Nigerian Government from Britain in 1951, and later by Ghana and Western Nigeria from Eastern Nigeria in 1952 and 1953. Even so, Northern Nigeria continued on a different path, as, for quite different reasons, did Sierra Leone; and today, freed altogether from the constraints of colonial rule and of the struggle for independence there is nothing to prevent each country or each distinctive ethnic group within a country from attempting to blend ancient local custom with modern imported practice so far as this may be useful.

GEOGRAPHY (physical and human) can be another great influence on the shaping of local government. Mountains and deserts must obviously impose their stamp on the way people are governed and administered, but these are of no great account in the more populated parts of West Africa (though parts of the Benue-Plateau and North-Eastern States of Nigeria are more inaccessible than many Nigerians realize). Rivers more directly determine the development of both 'provincial'[1] and local administration, and in the Niger Delta in particular local government will always have to adapt itself to the extraordinary patterns of

---

[1] Throughout this book the word 'provincial' is occasionally used as convenient shorthand for the variety of terms used in the three countries to denote political or administrative boundaries wider than local government—state, region, province, area.

land, swamp and water. But for the most part the geographical hazards of West Africa comprise nothing worse than the forest and jungle of the coastal belt, and the reasons why communications have been poor are economic rather than geographical—there has never been enough money to drive all-weather roads through the bush. And it is *communications* that are really the important geographical factor in local administration; they determine whether centralization is possible, irrespective of whether governments want it.

Even Britain was once a 'large' country, in that it could take a week in good weather to get from London to Newcastle or Exeter, and in those days the monarch or the Government had to rule through local people; the railways of the nineteenth century first began to weld the country into an easily administered whole, but it is interesting that the current pattern of local government (though it is admittedly now in its final years) was designed before the days of the motor-car or telephone, which is one of the contributory reasons why it is now thought necessary to reduce some 1,200 local authorities to a quarter of that number; for today it is possible to speak instantly to anyone in any part of the land and to reach the capital city from Newcastle or Exeter in a few hours.

In exactly the same way Nigeria, Ghana and Sierra Leone have 'shrunk' with remarkable suddenness. In recent memory Nigeria, for example, was effectively administered by 'Residents', provincial agents of the central colonial government, who performed an essential function if orderly government was to proceed at all. As communications improved they became correspondingly less necessary, until finally they became superfluous, because the headquarters of governments were so readily accessible. But when, for example, the Western Region of Nigeria included the Mid-West, the Resident Warri was performing a more vital function than the Resident Ibadan, because Warri was a long way from Regional Headquarters and could indeed be cut off for long periods in the rains. All-weather roads and above all the aeroplane have diminished distance, but West African communications by road, rail and telephone are still indifferent by international standards, and this fact must continue to affect local government for many years to come. In the main it should tend to enhance its importance, since as a general principle the worse the communications in any given area the greater the need for decentralization through devolution.

Human geography—the pattern of population—also has a direct influence on local government, and one which changes with the growth and shifts of population, and with the drift from rural areas to the towns. In the countries of the third world in particular the differences between local government in the rural areas and the large cities are so great that it is difficult to write about them both in general terms. Urban and rural authorities differ not only in their constitution, membership and staff but in their principal *purpose*, a point to which we return at the end of this chapter. Big cities the world over tend to produce a common type of man—the wage earner and commuter— and a common set of problems—sanitation, slum clearance, housing, transport, traffic, amenities. Administrators, doctors and engineers from Singapore, Chicago, Bombay, Lagos and Sheffield would quickly find common ground. By contrast, rural areas in the third world, though they have the common basic need of development, are more highly individualistic. Physical terrain, agricultural potential and, not least, social structure, all of which must influence local administration, have innumerable shades of difference.

There are of course the small towns, or the farming areas adjacent to the cities, where these extremes of difference do not apply with such force. But broadly speaking local government in Freetown, Accra and Lagos is utterly different in constitution and function from local government in a typical rural area in the northern parts of Sierra Leone, Ghana and Nigeria. Population, both in its ethnic or tribal origin and in its disposition on the map, is an important factor in the ecology of local government.

SOCIOLOGY means the science or study of the things which determine the way people live—their laws and customs, their family groupings and habits, their patterns of authority and power. So far as local government is concerned, these mean less in the cities than in the rural areas and they will mean less in a hundred years than they mean today, for there is a universal 'western' and urban influence at work in municipal affairs. Today, however, they are of great importance.

Ostensibly the 'natural rulers' of West Africa have less power than they had even a decade ago. This is partly because British colonial governments sustained and even increased their power both as a matter of principle and necessity, and British influence has gone; and partly because the existence of natural rulers is thought by the successor African governments to be against the main current of political thought in a world in which everybody suddenly knows what everybody else is doing. Thus the chiefs in Ghana were stripped of their power during Dr Nkrumah's régime, and even the great power of the Northern Nigerian emirs is being eroded by administrative decentralization. But the *influence* of natural authority, whatever the outward trappings of power, has not greatly diminished outside the larger cities, and in Ghana, as we shall see, the chiefs have regained statutory recognition in the new local government law.

We shall return to this subject in the concluding chapter, but the immediate point is that the shape of local government must clearly be affected by whether power has traditionally rested in, for example, a monarch and his court, as with the Ashantehene; the head of a powerful hierarchy, such as an emir; the personification of group will, such as an oba or paramount chief; or whether it has been diffused among elders and councils, as, broadly speaking, with the Ibo people.

Closely involved with traditional authority is the ownership or trusteeship of land, since progress, which is the one common purpose of local government in city and country alike, cannot take place without changing and improving the use to which land is put, or developing it for the public good. Traditional authority, moreover, cannot always be confined to the present earthly bearers of authority, for in many places ancestors have an important influence on current affairs.

Family, kinship group and tribe, and the complex relationships of dependence that arise from them and within them, have also to be embodied in local government. In western countries a man's standing *vis-à-vis* his local authority turns on whether he has lived in it long enough to pay his rates; in most of West Africa it is a much more personal matter. The deliberations of family, clan and tribal councils are at least as important in public affairs as those of statutory authorities, and local government must be shaped in such a way that there is some accord between the two.

These sociological factors vary very greatly from one ethnic group to another, even between one clan of the same ethnic group and another, and certainly between one religion and another. Islam, wherever it happens to be the dominant faith, imposes some semblance of uniformity, since it is a religion that does not discriminate between the spiritual and the secular but offers a code of behaviour in family relationships, governmental authority and spiritual discipline; for want of a better word it provides a common ethos. Otherwise the variety is bewildering, and probably greater than in other parts of the world. The controversial word 'tribe', though inappropriate to such large ethnic groups as Yoruba and Ibo, whose numbers exceed those of several independent states, does denote something peculiar to Africa, namely the many small groups whose languages and cultures are quite distinct.

Different societies reflect, among other things, different degrees of authoritarianism and egalitarianism, of dependence on the spirits of ancestors and on the spirit of progress, and this is clearly important in trying to establish 'democratic' local government.

The nature of POLITICS in any particular country must also have great influence on how local government develops.

In parliamentary democracies it tends to be pragmatic, i.e. it is based on practical work which it is thought can better be done locally than centrally, rather than on a political theory or philosophy; and although political parties are active in local authorities quite large areas of their work are non-political. Thus in Britain and Northern Europe parties oppose each other on matters which have a genuine political content, but do not range themselves into government and opposition on completely rigid lines, and over a wide range of non-contentious matters they are indistinguishable; majority and minority parties, may, for example, both be represented on working committees. Indeed, in the smaller authorities in Britain, whose work is politically uncontentious, party politics are hardly discernible, and councillors may stand for election as 'independents', relying only on their personal local reputation.

Local government in parliamentary democracies has also a greater or lesser degree of freedom from central government control, though there is no general rule about this. In Britain, as we have said already, local government historically preceded central government in many matters that are now considered important, and they used to have very great freedom of action. In the last thirty or forty years, however, this freedom has been greatly restricted, partly because of the need to impose uniform standards on a small but highly populated country, partly because central government has come to pay more and more of the bills through financial grant aid. The municipalities of Sweden and West Germany on the other hand still raise most of their own revenue and now have very much more autonomy than those in Britain. These, however, are questions of degree. What is general is that some kind of local autonomy and some kind of working relationship with political opponents are characteristic of local government in the parliamentary democracies.[2]

In one-party states, however, or states under military government, different considerations apply. One-party states usually exist because foreign, inherited forms of democracy have failed to take root, being alien to traditional concepts of government; or more positively because single parties are best suited to build nations out of weak, divided, artificial political entities. Military régimes exist to stop the gap in circumstances where civilian politics have broken down completely. In either event the overriding aim of government is unity, and there are many instances, in East Africa rather than in West, where local government has been suspect because it could be divisive. The conditions of parliamentary democracy being absent, questions of autonomy and pragmatism hardly arise. The aim of local government must be to further the aims of central government, and local discretion must be very narrowly restricted. 'Local administration' is perhaps a more apt description than local government, a point to which we shall return from time to time.

In Communist states, of course, local government is identified completely with the central organization of the Party. Its purpose, in the absence of a 'private sector', is the furtherance of development—agricultural, industrial, social and political, within the terms of Communist ideology.

Finally, local government must be seen against an ECONOMIC background. The British forms of local government with which West Africa experimented for some years were inappropriate for a number of reasons, one of which

---

[2] These remarks apply to those countries with what we called on p. 18 the 'Anglo-Saxon' tradition of local administration. In France and the countries which adopt her hierarchical kind of administration they have, of course, no application.

was the assumption that their main purpose was to translate *existing wealth* into social services, which would have an equalizing tendency as between rich and poor. But too often there was no existing wealth and everybody was poor. To achieve credibility local government had to go one stage further back and *create* wealth, i.e. assist in local economic development.

In the advanced democracies where there is a capitalist or a mixed economy (as indeed there is in anglophone West Africa) the idea of economic development as an aim of local government is alien. Agricultural or industrial, it is largely in the sphere of competitive private enterprise. The state may play a regulatory rôle or may be responsible for a limited number of nationalized industries, which are either natural monopolies or public utilities. But local authorities play no direct rôle at all. The most that could be said about local authorities in Britain is that they may sometimes provide the basic opportunities, such as land for factories or river frontage for docks and wharves, and the public services to support them; but the actual development is not their affair. Their business is to collect revenue from a local tax, called a rate (on property), and with the help of central government to provide schools, health services, public works, transport, markets and a wide range of amenities.

In West Africa the same may be said of large towns, except that their resources in money and staff are pitifully inadequate for such purposes; but in the rural areas it would be idle to pretend that local councils could from their own resources achieve very much that was significant in addition to what is already provided by the field agencies of government departments. Increasingly the view is held that rural local government is meaningless unless it is assisting in economic development—creating wealth which in the more distant future may yield the tax revenue from which social services can ultimately be financed.

There is admittedly some confusion of thought over what constitutes 'development'. Often the word is construed to mean anything that was not there before, irrespective of whether it is revenue-earning or a liability on existing revenues. Unfortunately the most popular forms of development—schools and health centres—are a heavy recurrent liability and produce no immediate return; their return lies in the improved health and education of the next generation. Markets and abbatoirs are other popular projects which pay their way as public utilities but cannot be said to *add* to wealth. The kind of developments which are most likely to produce returns in a near future are unfortunately the least popular—investment in improved agriculture, fisheries, drainage and irrigation and village industry.

But whatever form development may take it is increasingly the dominant consideration of governments when they are planning local government legislation. An extreme example is provided by the South-Eastern State of Nigeria, which has abolished local government under that name and substituted a form of 'development administration' (p. 183), which seeks to shift the emphasis from revenue-incurring to revenue-earning projects, and to leave the former to the central government exclusively. Against this background local government is increasingly thought of as a local development agency, playing an allotted part in a development programme which relatively little choice or discretion of its own.

From what we have now said about the influence on local government of history, geography, sociology, politics and economics it might seem that forms of local government are pre-determined by circumstances, and that national governments, in legislating for local administration, are simply agents for external forces. This is far from being true—the experience of the last twenty years tells us all too clearly that Governments can and will decide the form that local government should take. Unfortunately they have often swum against the tide, or misread the direction of the tide, and have established systems that did not accord with historical, geographical, sociological, political or economic realities. The lessons of these twenty years are now being digested, and already there are signs of a willingness to abandon the safe harbour of precedent for a voyage into the unknown.

CHAPTER 3

The Function of Local Government

IF we start, as we do in West Africa, from the fact that field agencies of Government directly provide roads, public works, schools, hospitals, agricultural services and much else besides, what is there left for local authorities to do—especially when, as in Sierra Leone and Ghana, there is the intermediate agency of the Province or Region? How is the work to be shared out? What should the central government devolve on to someone else? Putting it in its simplest terms, who is to do what, and why?

There is no universal answer to these questions. History, and the other influences which we discussed in the last chapter, provide different answers for different countries, and there is little point in describing what happens without discussing why it happens in that particular way. In Britain education is administered wholly by local authorities, but there is no reason why it should not be administered centrally; hospitals are controlled by regional boards of nominated members, but there is no reason why they should not be run by the larger local authorities, as they used to be; public assistance was for centuries dispensed by the parish, later by the larger local authorities, now by a national board working through a network of government offices which have nothing to do with local government. The explanation of why these arrangements exist, and why from time to time they have changed, would take us deep into history, sociology and the rest, with no particular enlightenment to the West African reader.

It might, however, be useful to dwell for a moment on the particular example of education, because in Britain in the past and in many parts of Africa today responsibility has been 'concurrent'; that is to say, a higher authority has been responsible for secondary education and a lower authority for primary.

In Britain all education other than university education has been a local authority responsibility since 1902, and the division as between secondary and primary was between the county and county borough councils on the one hand and certain district councils on the other. This ceased with the Education Act 1944, in the belief that it is wrong educationally and administratively for responsibility for a child's education to be split half way through his school career. An interesting point that we may notice in passing, since it illustrates our general theme, is that in New Zealand, a country of British stock and with a strong British tradition, education is administered directly by the Government. The geographical factor, especially that of small population, proved stronger than the historical or sociological, and today a New Zealander visiting Britain is surprised to find that the Department of Education and Science provides no schools, employs no teachers and designs no syllabus, but confines itself to broad strategic policy and to paying half the cost. The British reliance on local government to administer education is indeed exceptional and derives from nineteenth-century history.

In many parts of anglophone Africa, where education is the overriding interest of all classes of the community, the native authorities of colonial days and the local authorities of today have shown their eagerness to build primary schools and their willingness to make sacrifices to do so. Thus there has emerged the administrative pattern of divided responsibility that had been discredited in the British Act of 1944—the local authority primary school and the government secondary. It was a useful development in Africa, because it gave local councils a constructive job to do which had the enthusiastic backing of public opinion, and it got schools going where they did not exist. On the other hand the local councils' resources were very

limited and there was comparatively little that they could
do unaided—even in the primary schools which they built
the Government often had to pay the teachers. This divided
responsibility continues in many African countries, but
there are signs that some Governments are having second
thoughts about it.

The point was made in generalized terms in one of the
basic documents of governmental reconstruction in Ghana,
preceding the present Constitution. What is usually called
the Mills-Odoi Report,[1] to which we shall refer again in
a later chapter, had this to say when discussing the allocation of functions to local authorities:

". . . responsibility for single and closely related functions
ought not to be divided between two or more agencies . . .
except when a vertical control is exercised in a supervisory way."

But if vertical control is exercised in a supervisory way
it is difficult to make a distinction between local government and the field organization of a Ministry.

This brings us back to one of the central themes of this
book—how much devolution is possible, and is there some
halfway stage between devolution and deconcentration in
which 'local government' can survive in any meaningful
way? At this point it may be useful to recapitulate the
restraints which West African circumstances impose upon
devolution.

In the western democracies which we tend to take as the
yardstick of comparison it is possible for governments to
decide what they will do themselves and what they will
delegate to local authorities or other agencies on strictly
rational grounds. They do not always *act* rationally,
because they are as conditioned as anyone else by what
we have called their own ecologies—they cannot throw
off their traditions and circumstances any more easily than
Ghana or Nigeria. On the other hand in the countries of

[1] Report of the Committee on the Structure and Remuneration
of the Public Service in Ghana, December 1967. Para. 32.

West Africa there are some special restraints on devolution which arise from their recent isolation from the modern world and their entry into it during the twentieth century as colonial dependencies. We have mentioned them before in passing, but it may be helpful to summarize them here.

First, the fact that pre-literate and pre-scientific peoples were governed by European powers meant that the central government was exceptionally powerful and that the apparatus of modernization was imposed from a central point upon people who took very little active part in it. Except for the work of the Christian missions modernization came from government departments working through a provincial and district organization. Their field agencies, essential when things had to be done *for* people, came to be something of an obstacle when the time came for things to be done *by* people. In other words it is now difficult for local communities, coming into the picture after fifty years of departmental government, to find their feet, since the knowledge, the skill, the machinery and the money are so largely concentrated in central government hands. No one, black or white, is ever disposed to give up power voluntarily, and central departments tend to hold on to what they have got, which is nearly everything.

The result has been that administrative, professional and technical *competence* have been unduly concentrated in one place—the central government service. In western local authorities the calibre of staff is at least equal to that of the civil service. An English town clerk or city engineer is as highly qualified and as highly paid as a senior civil servant, and the professional expertise to be found even in a rural district council may be equivalent to that which could be found in a whole African province. This, then, is the first restraint on devolution—that without a considerable transfer of resources away from central to local government what can be devolved is limited to what can be done with little money or skill.

Second, devolution is limited by the need to work towards national development plans in which local authorities must play an ancilliary rôle, or in which their margins of discretion must be tightly restricted, if the overall plan is to succeed. There are two sides to this, since national plans cannot succeed without local co-operation, but this does not alter the fact that the area of devolution is small.

Third, devolution is exceptionally circumscribed by political expediency. The political temperature is higher in West Africa than in the western democracies and for some time to come, until national unity is secure and the possibility of secessions, *coups* and internal disaffection has disappeared, the devolution of power and the encouragement of local independence must be treated circumspectly. These dramatic possibilities may seem far removed from the mundane tasks of local government, but local government in a full sense cannot exist without a degree of local independence, and in the heightened political atmosphere differences that in England might result in mere political argument could in West Africa result in bloodshed. The point is perhaps best apprehended if it is remembered that quasi-independent local authorities may be opposed politically to the central government. In England at any moment half the major local authorities are controlled by the Labour Party under a Conservative Government or by the Conservative Party under a Labour Government. A good deal of political maturity and restraint are needed to keep the inherent conflict within the bounds of discussion and persuasion.

In the light of such considerations as these, can we say in terms of general principle what services ought to be devolved by central to local government rather than being provided by central agencies? This is perhaps a 'European' type of question, because it starts from the assumption that the main purpose of local government is to provide 'services', which in West Africa could well be open to question. It will perhaps be helpful to get a quite different point of view on the function of local government from another part of the world, but before doing so, and since

British thinking has so greatly conditioned the development of local government in West Africa, let us have a look at a typical British analysis, much read and quoted by students in West Africa even today.[2]

In this the work of local government is defined in terms of three groups of services—the environmental, the protective and the social. Even in English terms this analysis has become outdated. Contemporary problems of the 'environment' such as strategic physical planning, the traffic explosion and many forms of pollution—have become primarily national. The protective services include the police, whose administrative boundaries now largely ignore those of local government, and the fire services, which were nationalized during the Second World War and whose operational control is no longer local; while one of the most important of the social services, hospitals, was taken away from local government over twenty years ago.

For the developing world much of this is meaningless. Only public sanitation, one of the 'protective' group of services, can be said universally to be the responsibility of local communities. The unromantic subjects of refuse, sewage, drains, public cleansing, pure water and pest and disease control have been the foundation of local government everywhere. Almost everything else is a matter of argument, so far as its administrative setting is concerned.

By way of a complete contrast to the British type of analysis it is refreshing, and may be constructively useful, to turn to a system of decentralization which owes nothing to European concepts, the 'basic democracies' of Pakistan.[3]

Under the British Raj local administration was com-

---

[2] *The English Local Government System*, by J. H. Warren.

[3] For the substance of what follows the author is indebted to Mr A. K. Pickering of the Institute of Local Government Studies at Birmingham University. It is also included in an article written by the present author in the *Quarterly Journal of Administration* of the Institute of Administration at the University of Ife, Vol. V, No. 2, January 1971.

pounded of the mixture, familiar in British dependencies, of French practice and British principles. Whatever the nation-building virtues of the Raj may have been they did not comprehend close contact between governors and governed, for in India under the British the village peasant might have passed a lifetime in ignorance of any act of Government.

The initial purpose of the basic democracies was therefore communication. This was established, successfully, by an electoral chain which reached down to the so-called primary constituency of some 800–1,000 individuals. The penultimate link in this chain, the Union Council (rural), Town Committee (small urban) or Union Committee (municipal), with populations of the order of 10,000, was to be the effective agency for local government, though there was indirect representation through three further links in the chain ('Tehsil' or 'Thana', District and Division) which bound central and local government together. Indeed, shortly after their creation, the Union Councils became an electoral college for the formal choice of the President of Pakistan.

But electoral links, though they may help to solve the problem of communication, are not in themselves purposeful. Purpose was introduced by giving legal powers to the new basic democracies in the rural areas to levy taxes and carry out programmes of rural development, thus formalizing and regulating work previously done under the former Village Aid community development programmes. Over the next three years the material results of local government were impressive. Numerous roads, flood protection embankments, irrigation canals, village schools and other projects were built, often to quite a high standard of construction. It was this achievement that led the Government in 1962 to the idea of using basic democracies as a new machine for development and to supplement their efforts by substantial grants from the Public Sector funds. This was the first step towards making rural local government in Pakistan the principal agent for creating rural employment and increasing agricultural production. Between 1963 and the present-day allocations for the Rural Works Programme, as it is called, have increased steadily. At the same time the increasing power of the basic democracies has led to a greater measure of control over the field programmes of the technical departments of Government. At the time of writing the rural basic democracies control almost 10% of the Public Sector expenditure of the country.

Apart from these political and economic rôles the basic democracies have direct responsibility in two other areas of great importance in Pakistan, the administration of justice and family planning. In 1961 two ordinances, the Conciliation Courts Ordinance and the Muslim Family Laws Ordinance, gave them a large measure of judicial power. Under the first a number of civil and criminal cases were placed exclusively within the jurisdiction of basic democracies. Under the second the basic democracies were given wide powers to protect the rights and privileges of Muslim women and children. As a result of these ordinances an enormous burden of outstanding litigation was removed from the magistrates' courts. Cases which under the old system involved lengthy and often ruinously expensive processes were settled out of hand in the village. A sample survey of 1963–64 of 10,325 cases dealt with by 331 union councils showed that 85% of civil and 84% of criminal cases had been settled by the basic democracies. Further the survey showed—in rejection of charges of incompetence made by opponents of the system—that in the 15% of cases referred to the Appellate Courts the judgment of the basic democracies was upheld in over 70%.

As to family planning, it is difficult to exaggerate its importance to the development of Pakistan in the rest of the century, and in consequence the importance of basic democracies as the key agents of communication, motivation and local organization. In the crudest economic terms the position is that if the family planning programme were to achieve only one-tenth of its objectives by 1985 it would still have made a greater contribution to development than could be achieved by complete success in all other development programmes.

There is no suggestion, in making this long digression, that something which has been successful in Pakistan has any necessary relevance to West Africa, Indeed, it would be an interesting exercise to look back to the five constituent elements of what we called the ecology of local government to see what are the resemblances and differences between the Asian and African continents. Possibly only the need for economic development is held in common; there are certainly wide differences in history, geography, sociology and politics. The justification for discussing Pakistan, apart from its inherent interest, lies first in the fact that conventional ideas of the functions of local government, as derived in West Africa largely from British text books, are thrown overboard; and second that they offer at least a partial solution to the problem of combining deconcentration, which is the more effective pattern if scarce resources are to be employed to the best advantage, with devolution, which is necessary if the the will of the mass of the people is to be engaged; for though this is largely an exercise in devolution the more expensive resources come from the various points in the parallel government chain of command. But quite apart from their productive efforts, which need resources, they are there to foster social and political education.

With Africa rather than the Indian sub-continent in mind, let us revert to general principles. We have discussed the kind of responsibilities which governments have customarily delegated to local authorities, and the special difficulties which in Africa restrain governments from following their example without reservation. There has, however, been a missing factor in the argument, namely the size and population of the local authorities to whom it is proposed to delegate, for it is meaningless to discuss the functions of local authorities without also discussing the areas within which those functions are to be discharged.

The two are quite inseparable, and they present us with the central dilemma of local government in any country where it is practised, namely that there is always a conflict between efficiency, which generally tends to point to large units, and local democracy, which always tends to point to small ones. The problem can be summarized as follows:

The size, and more particularly the population, of a local authority determines its revenue; this in turn will determine what it is capable and what it is not capable of doing; moreover some of the functions of local authorities can be efficiently and economically administered over a small area, whereas others require a large one; as a further complication, some of those which need only a small area may come to need a larger one, as technical efficiency grows; consequently the administering authority may have to combine with others, in order to become bigger, or alternatively lose the administration of such functions altogether and allow them to be administered by a larger authority, such as a provincial, regional or national government. A related problem is that some functions which *can* be discharged satisfactorily over a small area (e.g. a town) nevertheless need highly qualified staff, which a small authority cannot afford.

In any country in the world this problem arises—that different functions need different areas for their economical and efficient administration. Unless, therefore, there is to be a separate authority for every function there is bound to be a compromise between what is most efficient and economical on the one hand and what is likely to be acceptable to the local people on the other. Even if—to carry the argument to an absurd point—a separate authority were to be established for every function, the problems of overlapping that this would create would outweigh the advantage gained from the best administration of each individual function.

The various ways in which compromises have been made in West Africa in the 1950s and 1960s—the formative years —will be briefly discussed in a later chapter. We may conclude this one by asking why so much thought and effort have been put into local government in the past, and why (as we shall see from the concluding chapters) so much is now being put into reconstructing something which has on the whole failed to live up to expectations. The answer lies in the fact that in West Africa local 'representative democracy' is an extraordinarily persistent idea. It has often failed miserably in the past, killed by incompetence and corruption, but it offers a good example of the saying 'it's dead but it won't lie down'. The Governments of Sierra Leone, Ghana and Nigeria, after their disappointing experiences of the 1960s, were at perfect liberty to have done with it, and to substitute central hierarchical administration. They have deliberately chosen not to do so. We shall look briefly at the position in mid-1971 (the time of writing) in due course, but we may say in anticipation that although local government is to be reconstituted in the somewhat different form of 'local administration', i.e. it is to be woven more closely into the texture of central government, the functions that it is proposed to delegate to locally elected councillors are as wide-ranging as before.

The ultimate logic of local government is that every public service should be administered by the smallest possible unit. For electricity, for example, this might be the whole country; for public works, the province of a country; for education, a joint board of several councils.

Some years ago the Government of what was then Western Nigeria did some serious research into the size of area and population which was suitable for the administration of the major social services, having in mind the possibility of creating *ad hoc* 'service areas'. They came to the conclusion that the optimum area over which to administer education was one which contained between 550 and 600 primary schools, taking account of the staff that was needed for teaching, inspection and maintenance; and that an area which contained less than 100 primary schools would be both uneconomic and inefficient. They applied similar tests to the public health service, and concluded that the optimum was one which employed not less than fifteen health inspectors; one factor which they took into account here was the need to have a big enough staff employed by one agency to allow for internal promotion; the lack of opportunity for promotion in the service of small local authorities is one of their most disheartening features, and one which virtually prevents them from employing staff of any real calibre. Tests of this kind can be applied to all the major services with which local authorities are associated. This is not the place to examine them in any further detail, but two observations can be made about them; first, that only the few biggest authorities came anywhere near the minimum standard for efficiency; second, that the method of approach is in itself of great significance—(*a*) what is the optimum area for administering a certain service? (*b*) how near can we get to this optimum, bearing in mind the other factors which have to be taken into account, such as traditional areas, local loyalties, communications and, as always, politics? For local government areas can never achieve the ideal—always there must be a search for a compromise between what will satisfy the people and what will provide efficient and progressive administration.

For a wide range of minor services such as sanitation, minor roads, markets, rural water supplies and so on, the natural agency is a fairly local kind of council at what has usually been called the 'district' level, and it is here that local government is likely to be judged as to its failure or success. Without pre-judging the issue—for several years must pass before it is possible to form a judgment—it is always possible that it could fail, through no fault of its own, because enough resources were not assigned or transferred to it by central government. It cannot be expected to find its own feet as it did in wealthy England of the nineteenth and early twentieth centuries, a time of buoyant revenues and rich local resources.

If this should happen it might be that local government will find its real vocation at the level of the village, partly as a forum of opinion, representing the people to the Government and the Government to the people, and partly as an agency for community development, i.e. for the relatively simple kind of self-help which does not require the support of staff, equipment, offices and ambitious budgets, but which on the other hand ebbs and flows unless it can rely on modest but reliable resources and on statutory support. Indeed, many people think that until West African countries in general are rich enough in men and money to equip a sophisticated form of local government with the resources that it needs the village is the right place for it to begin.

The important thing, especially in view of the history of the 1950s, is to 'cut the coat according to the cloth', and not to give local authorities powers on paper that they can never hope to exercise in practice. The first local government laws in 1950–54 were passed in a state of urgency and euphoria. Complicated political motives were behind them—destroying indirect rule through the chiefs (the hall-mark of colonialism), creating local machinery for national political parties, placating local interests and handing out patronage. It is significant that national leaders, later to become Presidents and Prime Ministers, all took the ministerial portfolios of local government in their early days of power. In this atmosphere practical realities were not seriously considered, and powers were given to local authorities which they had no hope of using; it is no good giving a local council the power to build a hospital if its resources would be strained by building a bicycle shed.

In a word, local authorities were first created for political and prestige reasons, and it was then necessary to decide what they ought to do. In the light of hindsight it would have been better to have made an inventory of resources and then to have considered how they could best be deployed and how far they would stretch. Was there room for province, district and village? Or only for two of the three, and if so which? Or possibly only for one? Or none?

CHAPTER 4

Local Authorities

1. THEIR CONSTITUTIONAL BASIS

BY 'local authorities' we mean bodies which are set up by statute to discharge certain duties and to exercise certain powers, including the power to tax. 'Local councils', which are discussed in the next chapter, mean very nearly the same thing, since legal authority is vested in elected councillors; but it is worth preserving the distinction, so that in this chapter we can discuss the *institution* of local government, and in the next the *people* who operate the institution.

Local authorities are normally created by Acts of Parliament, by whatever name these may be known, and their powers and duties are defined in departmental legislation. A partial exception to this is to be found in Ghana today, where the Constitution itself provides that there shall be certain kinds of local authority and even outlines their membership; but a subsequent Act of Parliament has, of course, been required to give precision to these requirements and to furnish local government with a statutory basis within the Constitution.[1]

There are various ways in which particular local authorities come to be established and given specific powers and duties. In Britain a principal Local Government Act defines a number of local authorities by name, specifies their membership and gives them a constitutional basis. The principal Act does not, however, allocate functions.

[1] See p. 172.

These derive from other legislation not concerned with local government as such but with social services such as education, housing, public health, roads and transport, markets, libraries and museums and a host of others. Thus Education Acts lay duties on 'counties' and 'county boroughs' and Housing Acts on 'county districts'. The result of this is that all local authorities bearing the same name have the same functions. In West Africa the method has been somewhat different—Local Government Acts have specified the kinds of local authority that may exist and the full range of functions which local authorities as such may discharge. But the allocation of particular functions to particular local authorities has been made through the more individual device of an 'Instrument', whereby a Minister may use his discretion to allocate whatever functions may seem appropriate to any type of local council in the light of local circumstances. Thus the powers of one 'divisional' council, for example, might differ slightly from those of another, or 'district' councils might have relatively weaker or stronger powers in different parts of a 'region'. It is a more flexible arrangement than the British one and has certain advantages.

In the last chapter we discussed some of the problems that arise in deciding *what* functions should be delegated to local authorities, but something more may appropriately be said in this one about *how* they may be allocated.

Duties and Powers

First, a distinction is often made between mandatory (i.e. compulsory) duties and permissive (i.e. optional) powers. Thus in British legislation counties and county boroughs *must* provide primary and secondary education; they *may* provide nursery school education. District councils *must* provide housing; they *may* provide swimming baths. Most powers in West African legislation were permissive, for the obvious reason that compulsion must be governed by available resources, and government have not been generous in grant-aiding local authorities to the extent that would enable them to discharge, under compulsion, a very wide range of functions.

Ultra Vires

Second, there is an important legal doctrine that may restrict the discretionary activities of a local authority—that of *ultra vires*, the effect of which is that local authorities may do only those things which an Act specifically says they may do. This in in contrast to the position of an individual person in a free society, who may do anything he likes unless the law says he may not do it. British local government has been very greatly restricted by *ultra vires* and for a long time there has been a school of thought that has held that it should be relaxed. Its effect is that the legal officers of local authorities must constantly watch to see that their councils do nothing that the law does not permit, for if they do members of the council may be 'surcharged', i.e. made to meet out of their own pockets the cost of such unauthorized expenditure. When major local authorities have wished to go outside the provisions of existing Acts of Parliament they have had to promote Private Bills seeking special powers. This is slow and costly, but it has very commonly been done, so that the General Acts which govern all local authorities are supplemented by a great many Private Acts governing particular local authorities.

By contrast, the work of municipalities in West Germany and Sweden is based on the opposite doctrine of *intra vires*, i.e. they may spend their money on whatever activities they choose, providing that such activities are themselves legal and provided that there is no existing legislation which already allocates them to some other arm or agency of government.

Earlier West African legislation rested in general on the doctrine of *ultra vires*, but sometimes appeared to try to make the best of both worlds. That is to say the Acts spelt out in great detail what local authorities could legally do, but added an 'omnibus' clause at the end saying that they could do anything else that was designed to increase the prosperity and well-being of the neighbourhood, for example engaging in trading or commercial activities. However, as we have said repeatedly, this meant little in practice as their resources were generally so limited that they could only do the absolutely basic things. On the other hand 'open-ended' legislation is always potentially troublesome unless very carefully drawn, as it may encourage irresponsibility. There have been cases, for example, where councils have decided to spend public money on expensive lawsuits about chieftaincy matters, which had nothing to do with the purposes of local government law.

Law and Order

One matter in which West African local authorities have differed from the British, and more closely resembled the French, is in their *general* responsibility for law and order. They have, of course, *specific* powers to deal with natural nuisances such as fires and man-made nuisances such as brothels, gambling, begging, hawking and noise. But there has always been in addition a general duty laid upon all local authorities, which cannot be listed as a specific function or defined with any precision; that is the duty generally to assist in maintaining order and good government. The Nigerian laws went further and made it an obligation on every council and every individual member of a council to do their best to prevent crime or breaches of the peace, and individual councillors could be punished if they failed to take certain steps, such as reporting to the proper authorities, and carrying out the orders of a police officer or justice of the peace as a result of this.

This responsibility for law and order used to be emphasized by the existence of local authority police forces and prisons, but in recent years these have become central responsibilities.[2] They were an inheritance from colonial

[2] At the time of writing the future of local authority police in the Northern States of Nigeria is under discussion.

administration when the 'native authority' was almost synonymous with the 'native court', and for many years after independence they served a useful purpose in supplementing the work of the Federal Police Force, especially in the proceedings of the customary courts and in routine work such as serving official documents and regulating traffic. Now, however, the tendency is to separate the administration of justice from the administration of services. Local authorities may, however, be responsible for maintaining the local court, which was formerly the arrangement in Britain. Unlike Britain, fines, fees and other court proceeds may form part of the revenues of councils and appear in estimates of income and expenditure.

By-Laws

Finally, although the councils of local authorities are for the most part 'deliberative' bodies—i.e. they decide local policies and see to their implementation—they also have minor legislative powers. Their decisions may involve the ordinary person in obeying their orders, and this would be impossible unless they had such powers and the ability to enforce them.

Accordingly local government legislation confers upon them the power to make 'by-laws', for which penalties are imposed if the by-laws are not obeyed.

It is not easy for amateur legislators like councillors to make proper by-laws, and the process is carefully safeguarded. No by-law of a local council can become effective until it has been approved by the Minister, and this provision is necessary for a number of reasons. First, the Government's legal advisers must make sure that the proposed by-law is *intra vires*, i.e. within the council's competence to make; second it must be in correct legal form; and finally it must not conflict with any other law or by-law, made by any legally constituted authority, within the area of the council's jurisdiction. Because of these difficulties it is the practice of governments to publish 'model' or 'adoptive' by-laws on subjects which are of common interest to large numbers of councils; it is then only necessary for the council to 'adopt' this particular by-law, and all the trouble over drafting and investigation is saved.[3]

The nature of most by-laws follows naturally from the functions of local authorities. If examples are required, in order to give a mental picture of the scope of local legislation, an old Western Nigerian Local Government Law is most helpful, as it gives a list of no fewer than thirty-nine matters, in five broad categories, on which by-laws may be made. We take a few typical examples from each:

Natural Resources

Controlling disease in trees, crops or plants; the movement of livestock; fencing; rules about cultivation.

Markets

Goods which may or may not be sold; rents and fees; inspection of produce offered for sale; weights and measures; maximum prices.

Roads and Transport

Obstruction of drains or watercourses; planting and destroying of trees; demolition of dangerous buildings; licensing of bicycles and carrying of lights; naming and numbering of streets; advertisements.

Public Order

Control of firearms, weapons, noise, gambling, begging, hawking, etc.

Miscellaneous

Licensing of entertainments, registration of births, deaths and marriages, intoxicating liquor.

---

[3] In the same way it is the practice to issue 'model standing orders' and 'model contracts'.

Contracts

Another activity which arises constantly from the ordinary work of a council is the award of contracts, either for buildings or for the purchase of goods. In order to prevent fraud by irresponsible councils, of which there has unfortunately been a great deal, these awards are controlled by governments, and large contracts have to be approved by the Minister, who makes certain that they have been put out honestly to tender, that the best tender is recommended for acceptance, and that councillors voting to award contracts have no personal or financial interest in them. In Western Nigeria and Ghana the maximum contract which a council may award on its own authority used to be £2,000 (£5,000 in Ghanaian municipalities); in Eastern Nigeria it was much lower.

2. THEIR RELATIONSHIP WITH EACH OTHER

Local authorities may assume a number of alternative patterns on the map. There may be one authority or several in any given place; where there is more than one their relationship may be of a superior-subordinate kind or it may be a parallel relationship of constitutional equality; or there may be joint boards or similar arrangements between adjacent authorities of the same status.

Single authorities or 'tiers'?

One of the great differences between local administration in France and Britain is that in France there is only one kind of 'local authority', the *commune*. Whether the area is rural, with a small and scattered population, or a vast city of the size of Marseilles, it is still for official purposes a *commune*. In Britain, on the other hand, there may be two or even three authorities operating in the same place; only in the large cities, known for local government purposes as 'county boroughs', is there just one self-contained authority. Elsewhere there may be two 'tiers' or levels of authority—the 'county' and the small towns or urban districts within its borders; or even three—the county, the rural district, and within the rural district the parish.[4]

Although complicated by historical influences (especially in its nomenclature), it is basically logical in that it recognizes that certain functions need to be discharged by large authorities, some by medium-sized ones, while others can be discharged by very small ones. The pattern can be seen most graphically by standing in the middle of an English village and looking round at the various things which local government provides. The churchyard, the village green, a local footpath, will probably be maintained by the parish council, which might also have constructed a village hall and car park. The small group of council houses on the other hand, and the sewage and drainage that serves them, will have been built by the rural district council; while the village school, if there is one, and the road on which you stand will be the responsibility of the county council, who will also be supplying clinics, libraries and other services in the local market town. There is in each case some correspondence between the resources required to provide and maintain these services and the financial resources of the various authorities responsible for them. There are, however, no such things as urban parishes, so that in the towns responsibility is divided only between the county and the town; while in the bigger cities (county boroughs, i.e. boroughs which have also the powers of a county) there is only one single authority responsible for everything.

Since the needs of the man in the village are being met by three different authorities it follows that each of them will want money from him in the form of local tax (which

[4] This is a description of the system as it will continue until, probably, 1974, when it will be superseded by a system of fewer and larger authorities, following the recommendation of the Royal Commission on Local Government which sat from 1966 to 1969. The new arrangements will, however, perpetuate a 'two-tier' system.

is a rate levied on property). But to save him having to pay three different rates the rate is consolidated and collected from him by the rural district, who will pass most of it to the county, whose services are the most expensive, and a very little to the parish, keeping the rest for its own purposes. Before this is done the county and the parish will have made a requisition (called a 'precept') for the money they require.

West African legislation in the 1950s followed the 'tier' system (outside the big cities), but it was never successful and had virtually crumbled away before the end of the '60s. By 1965, for example, there was only one kind of authority, the district, in Ghana; in Eastern Nigeria there were two, the 'county' and the 'local'; in Western Nigeria three nominally survived, the 'division', the 'district' and the 'local', but there had been so much alteration and fragmentation to meet local pressures that no coherent pattern remained.

In the light of hindsight it is easy to see that the system was too complicated, that it had no relevance to traditional forms, and that in particular the requirement that one local authority should collect the tax only to part with most of it to another, upon whom they might not look with favour, aroused deep suspicion and resentment. But although it was inevitable that such a complicated system should disintegrate, the way in which it did so leaves cause for regret. Again in the light of hindsight one can see that there was a case for large authorities, which could command enough financial resources to administer expensive services; or for small village authorities which were traditional and cohesive and could engage the peoples' support even if they could do nothing financially ambitious; ideally one could envisage the one supplementing the other. Unfortunately, because of local politics and the compromises they inevitably entail, the general tendency was to break away from the large authority, because it commanded no local loyalty, but to be dissatisfied with the small one because it lacked prestige, and so to make just the wrong sort of compromise by settling for the medium-sized district which failed to hit either target.

The difficulty in developing countries, which stands out more sharply than the same difficulty in Britain, is that the mass of people are not sufficiently informed to be able to think of local government at all in terms of areas suitable for efficient administration; while politicians, who *do* understand the problem, are too much swayed by the people on whom they depend for votes, and support small, uneconomical and out-of-date local council areas even when they know they are against the best interests of development. The ordinary man tends to see local government in terms of local feuds, traditional rivalries, and distrust of neighbouring towns or communities with whom he is unwilling to share his own resources, and whom he suspects of getting more than their fair share of benefits; not only does he not want his council to combine with others—he would like it to become still smaller; and the politicians often back him up. Probably the best solution would be to leave the 'natural' areas, in which peoples' local loyalties reside, untouched; to give them as much to do as possible; but not to give them powers and duties in connection with the major services on which the progress of West Africa depends—agriculture and natural resources, public education, public health or major public works. All governments want to avoid the enforcement of unpopular measures, not only for political reasons but because development will flow more smoothly if people are governed by consent; but in countries where there are such great extremes in the level of understanding they may have to be prepared to take their courage in both hands.

Joint Bodies

One compromise that has long been practised is the institution of 'Joint Committees' or 'Joint Boards'. Joint Committees, which were provided for in all the laws in West Africa, are a simple device. It was provided that 'councils may concur, with one or more other councils, in appointing from their respective members a joint committee of the councils for a purpose in which they are jointly interested', and such committees could be given delegated powers, other than legislative or financial powers. This enabled councils, by voluntary agreement, to deal with matters which cut across their boundaries or which they could better manage in co-operation; thus a joint committee might be responsible for a water supply which for reasons of local geography could provide water on both sides of a local government boundary line; or (except in Eastern Nigeria) there could have been a joint committee for managing a combined local police force.

Joint Boards, which were provided for in the Western Nigerian Law, were altogether more important bodies, and come very near to being a new kind of local authority in their own right. They could be established by voluntary agreement between councils, but normally they were created by Government action—'The Minister may *require* any two or more councils to establish a joint board for any purpose. . . .' They had their own Instruments defining their powers and duties, which must be approved by the Minister and gazetted; the 'contributing councils' appointed their own members, but once appointed they were not subject to their councils' direction, but held office on the board in their own right. Several of the 'local education authorities' in this Region were joint boards of councils, and not the councils themselves.

Here we see the same development that we noted in Britain—the creation of *ad hoc* boards, in the manner of the nineteenth century, for the purpose of performing a certain function which the local authorities individually are not capable of performing properly.

Once this principle is accepted—once, that is to say, it is admitted that the statutory local authorities are inadequate for their jobs—there is no reason why it should not be extended indefinitely, so that the structure of local government could be radically altered *within* the existing local government legislation. Indeed, Western Nigeria once considered extending it, so that the important services of education, public health and works could be administered by much larger bodies; though in the discussions that took place they were thought of as 'service authorities', i.e. new authorities for the purpose of performing one function only —rather than as joint boards as at present constituted. The difference would be more than a mere difference in name, as certain constitutional and staffing changes were contemplated; but all this disappeared in the events leading up to the civil war.

Subordinate or Parallel?

In the system we outlined earlier none of the authorities was subordinate or superior to another. They were simply responsible for doing different things. Ordinary people in West Africa found this difficult to realize for a number of reasons, partly because of tradition, both colonial and pre-colonial; partly because an authority with important powers seemed manifestly the superior of one with small powers; and partly because the payment of precept became confused in their minds with the payment of tribute. Should the system continue in the future, however, it is important to realize that the smallest local council is directly responsible to the Minister, and not to the district or divisional council in which it may be situated.

In this as in many other matters the Northern Region of Nigeria was exceptional. The Native Authority Law of 1954 provided for the establishment of subordinate authorities, which could take a number of different forms. In the first place the Law (sections 20–24) allows the Governor to establish subordinate native authorities in the full sense, and where this is done the subordinate authority must 'obey the orders of the native authority to which the Governor has directed that it shall be subordinate', but it may also exercise powers delegated to it by the superior authority. There are at present forty-nine subordinate native authorities in the Region. The Law does not in fact differentiate in any way between an NA and a subordinate NA and unless the superior authority restricts the powers or its subordinate by a published Order, the subordinate NA has the full powers of a native authority within the area of its jurisdiction. They are constituted in exactly the same way as native authorities, and they are most commonly found in the 'Federations', where the individual member authorities are subordinate to the Federation Council.

But the Law also allows (sections 54–5) the creation of administrative sub-areas within any native authority, and from the point of view of comparing Southern Nigeria, Ghana and Northern Nigeria these are of greater interest. Section 54 of the Law says that a native authority may 'divide the area under its jurisdiction . . . into districts, village areas, wards and such other administrative sub-areas as it may consider expedient', and goes on to say, in effect, that it may appoint district, village and ward heads. These heads constitute the most important difference between the North and elsewhere, so far as day-to-day administration is concerned.

It is sometimes thought that this kind of 'chain of command' is undemocratic, especially as the offices of heads are traditional, sometimes hereditary, and derive from an ancient and authoritarian system. It does not, of course, accord with twentieth-century bureaucratic concepts. On the other hand a traditional office was adapted to an increasingly representative form of local government, and there is no doubt that the district head is a modern administrator and an extremely efficient tax collector. He is peculiar to the emirates, and it not to be found, except in a very modified form, in what one might call the non-emirate states. Village headmen, on the other hand, are universal throughout the Northern States.

3. THEIR RELATIONSHIP WITH THE CENTRAL GOVERNMENT

Legally, as well as by convention, the 'central government', so far as local authorities are concerned, means 'the

Minister'; but in the circumstances of West Africa the ministerial presence is somewhat closer at hand, as a result of the deconcentration of government that we discussed in the first chapter. In Sierra Leone and Ghana central government is projected at the provincial and regional level. The Sierra Leone Province has no statutory council, but field officers of government are stationed at the three provincial capitals; the new Ghanaian Region, by contrast, is part of the Constitution and is overseen by a Regional Council with the definite function of overall planning; though mainly an elected body its chairman is the personal nominee of the Prime Minister, and for practical purposes it is the central government so far as the district councils are concerned. In Nigeria the central government in the present context means the governments of the twelve States, though as we shall see (p. 206) provincial administration has been retained in the North Eastern and North Central States.

But there is a local representative of the central government even nearer home in the person of an administrative officer—the lineal descendant of the old DO or DC of colonial days—who now has direct oversight of one or more local authorities. He differs a good deal from his expatriate predecessor. He is generally younger, and though as government agent he may technically be *primus inter pares* among his professional and technical colleagues he does not have the fortuitous prestige or superior rank of the old colonial DO, but is more like an outposted officer of the Ministry of Local Government. The immediate point is that the Minister has his representative on every local authority's doorstep.

It is widely believed in West Africa that local authorities are 'mere agents' of the central government. It is understandable that people should think this, but it was not the original intention, and if local councils had in earlier years behaved more responsibly they would probably be enjoying greater freedom from central government control than they do today. To a very large extent, both in Britain and West Africa, they enjoy the freedom they deserve.

The relationship between central and local government in Britain, like that between councillors and officials, is one which Africans tend to find puzzling and unsatisfactory. They want a straightforward answer to the question 'Which is master and which is servant?', and are dissatisfied with the answer 'Neither'. In law the control of local authorities by the central government is considerable, though not as great as in West Africa; in practice the influence of unwritten conventions and personal relationships greatly modifies this fact.

Administrative control takes many forms in Britain. One of them is *inspection*; most people have heard of Her Majesty's Inspectors of Schools, whose duty is to see that local education authorities are properly fulfilling their responsibilities under the Education Act; there are also Home Office inspectors, who do the same for police forces, fire brigades, safety regulations, etc. The formal purpose of these inspectors is to see that services which Parliament has given to local authorities to administer, but which also have a national implication, and for which the Government pays grants-in-aid, are being maintained at a minimum level of efficiency; their informal purpose is to assist and advise; for inspection, like so many other things, is subject to unwritten conventions, and need not take the form, as is frequently supposed in West Africa, of finding fault and exacting retribution; an inspector may equally well be a friendly adviser.

Another form of control is by what are usually called *default powers*, which means that if a Minister is not satisfied with the way in which a local authority is performing its functions he may make an order requiring it to do certain things by a certain time, and if it fails to do so he may take the powers away from it and exercise them himself, either directly or by appointing a new authority to do so.

Again, certain matters which are within the general

competence of local authorities nevertheless require *ministerial approval* before they are valid. Certain local authorities are responsible for building schools and houses; but they are required to submit the plans to the appropriate Ministry for approval, as the Government wants to make sure that certain standards are maintained throughout the country and that public funds are spent to the best advantage; for example, in the building of schools the Minister of Education will insist on certain *national*, not local, standards in such matters as design, space, ventilation, lighting, playgrounds, playing fields, equipment and so on. A more far-reaching control, but one on the other hand which throws great responsibilities on the local authority, is in the *submission of long-term schemes* to the Minister for development, e.g. in town and country planning and education.

Apart from these specific controls Ministers today have very considerable powers of *delegated legislation*. Most Acts of Parliament governing the services which local authorities administer deal only with broad principles; much of the detail is left to be filled in from time to time by 'the Minister', who is empowered under these Acts to make subsidiary legislation, in the form generally known as 'statutory instruments'.

But alongside these controls of inspection, default powers, ministerial approval, submission of schemes and delegated legislation, there is constant consultation of a less formal kind between ministries and local authorities, both through demi-official correspondence and personal discussion between civil servants on the one hand and chief officers of local authorities, chairmen of committees and representative councillors on the other.

The fact that most local authorities behave responsibly means that controls are kept to a minimum and consultation to a maximum, and hence there can grow up a *partnership* between ministries and local authorities. Partnerships can of course vary in degree, and there can be senior, junior or equal partners; the kind of partnership which exists between government departments and local authorities varies with the subject matter. For example, in housing the Government could be called the senior partner, since it provides most of the money and keeps a close control on siting, design and cost; the local authority's function is to select the tenants and maintain the houses in good condition. In providing many local amenities, on the other hand, the local authority is the senior partner, for the Government is not heavily involved financially and does not wish to exercise control in the national interest. In education the partnership could be called an equal one, since the Ministry of Education keeps a tight control on the building, design, equipment and cost of schools, but the local authority has real independent responsibility for what happens inside them, in relation to children, teachers and syllabus.

But looking at the picture as a whole, British local authorities can justify their claim to be 'quasi-autonomous'. They do not have to submit their financial estimates for approval, they are given wide discretion in the award of contracts and the appointment of staff; some services they manage in their full discretion, and even in those which they manage under close government control they are a good deal more than agents. (It *is*, incidentally, possible for a local authority to act simply as an agent of a central government department, e.g. in the construction of national trunk roads through the area of a county council; but this is not an important aspect of their work, and incidentally has no relevance to West Africa, where county councils or their equivalents would not be competent to build trunk roads.)

Why, then, since the local government laws of West Africa set out to emulate British practice, is the idea so deeply rooted that local authorities are no more than the agents of government? The answer is that after allowing the new local authorities an initial burst of freedom, governments have increasingly tightened the controls which originally existed and have introduced new ones; and they have done this because the financial irresponsibility, bribery and corruption of councils compelled them to do it, and not because they wanted to. It is this which accounts for the three kinds of control which local authorities most resent, and which do not exist in the British system—approval of estimates, approval of the award of contracts (over a modest amount) and approval of the employment of staff. Such controls need not, however, be permanent. One very significant event took place in Western Nigeria, where the Government decided to grant 'financial autonomy' to those councils which earned it by a good financial record, including a record of rate collection, over a period of years. This would have freed them from most government financial controls, though not of course from government audit.

The controls which we have outlined above as being characteristic of British local government could of course all be found in the West African local government laws, or alternatively in subsidiary (delegated) legislation or administrative instructions. So far as the principal laws are concerned they were most fully and explicitly set out in the Eastern Nigerian Law (Part III—'Powers of the Minister') and the Western Nigerian Law (Part XI—'General Powers of Supervision and Inspection'). The Ghana Local Government Act of 1961 included most of the same provisions, but was arranged rather differently. In the first place the Minister had wide powers to amend the Instrument establishing a council, though he could only exercise this power after giving the council concerned an opportunity to express its views, and after obtaining the approval of the President; this power allowed him to alter the council's functions and even gave him a considerable say in its internal arrangements. He could also alter the area of a local authority, though in this case only after a public enquiry had been held. There is no counterpart to controls of this kind in British local government, because the councils do not have individual Instruments—every council of a given status exercises the same functions, and alterations of this order would need legislation by Parliament.

The remaining powers of the Minister, in all three countries, are more familiar to British local government, from which indeed they were originally copied, and are largely concerned with councils which fail in their duties or responsibilities, i.e. they are default powers. Thus if a council fails to hold regular meetings, or is not using its revenues in a responsible way, or is manifestly corrupt, or is failing to levy and collect the rates, the Minister may dissolve it.

These controls sound very drastic, and may give the impression that local councils were entirely 'under the thumb' of the Minister. There is, however, nothing unusual in their existence, and any council in Britain which failed to carry out its responsibilities would be subject to similar discipline. What was unusual, and deplorable, was that experience made it necessary to give such disciplinary controls a prominent place in the law, and to exercise them fairly frequently. But this arose from a failure in the human element, and cannot be held as a criticism of the local government laws or of the institution of local government.

There is another important control, which will be found in any local government system in the world, namely *audit*. The accounts of local authorities must be audited by persons appointed by the Minister (usually the Government Auditor and his staff), and the auditors must consider not only the accuracy of the accounting but the legality of all expenditure; here we return to the legal doctrine of *ultra vires*, by which local authorities may only do those things which the law says they may do. If they spend money on a purpose which is not specified in their Instrument the auditors may disallow such expenditure, and the person or persons responsible for it may be 'surcharged' with the amount—that is, they may be compelled to pay it back out of their own pockets.

One of the most regrettable things about local government in West Africa, ever since its reorganization in the early 1950s, has been that the Government Auditors' offices have been understaffed and overworked, and have not been able to give the assistance to local council treasurers that they would have liked. For an auditor need not necessarily be an inspector whose arrival is dreaded, and who comes to find fault; indeed Government auditors would much rather play the rôle of teachers and helpers of local council treasurers; and treasurers, many of whom have had scant training for their work, would welcome such expert guidance; both sides would much prefer prevention to cure (or punishment). But such is the pressure on the auditors that they have frequently been more than a year behindhand with their work, so that they have only been able to study the accounts after mistakes or illegalities have been committed, and they have not been able to spend enough time at the councils' headquarters to act as teachers or advisers.

This is an appropriate point at which to introduce a wider topic—that of inspection and advice generally. Since the early 1950s local authorities have been called upon to undertake responsibilities of a kind which require maturity and experience, and to perform unfamiliar functions under complicated laws and regulations. It would have been reasonable, in these early years, to give them close inspection and support. Unfortunately these years coincided with the withdrawal, or at least the diminution, of control by the district officer or district commissioner; this arose partly from deliberate policy, and partly from a progressive shortage of administrative officers, caused to some extent by the departure of expatriates. The point is worth discussing a little more fully.

In the days of the native authorities 'Divisions' or 'Districts' (the name varied) were effectively administered by the DO (or DC), who was the local representative of the central government and its principal agent. NAs were slowly acquiring greater responsibilities, as they showed themselves fit for them, but the DO was the 'power in the land',

and NAS which were irresponsible, corrupt or inefficient could be effectively checked or controlled by him. The transition to 'local government', especially a system of local government modelled so closely on the British pattern, raised difficult questions of principle. In the first place, there was no one in the British system who corresponded to the DO—indeed, a local representative of the Government, exercising comprehensive powers, would be foreign and repugnant to British local government; secondly, it was the general intention that local authorities should *replace* the DO, and that elected representatives of the people should take over the control of local affairs which he previously exercised.

It is now apparent, however, that it is no longer the *intention* that local representatives of the central government should disappear. On the contrary, shortly after political independence the colonial Resident or Provincial Commissioner, who was a political and administrative officer in one, was replaced by two people—a politician (Commissioner) and a civil servant (Secretary) who stood to each other in a similar relationship to that of Minister and Permanent Secretary. In Northern Nigeria before the civil war, and in Sierra Leone they were accorded the status of Minister.

Such developments came to have a great influence on local government. The new Provincial Commissioner had no direct statutory control over local authorities, since his function was the much wider one of bringing the Government into closer touch with the people, explaining its policies and endeavouring to see that they were implemented; the dividing line between 'Government' and 'Party' was not, of course, always very clear-cut. The Provincial Secretary, on the other hand, had definite responsibilities for the local authorities—indeed in the former Eastern Nigeria he was in one of his capacities 'commissioner for local government', and in the old Northern Nigeria his responsibilities were equally specific.

The division of Nigeria into twelve States, the new Constitution for Ghana and the internal reforms in Sierra Leone have altered the pattern in detail, but the trend away from quasi-independent 'local government' and towards an integrated form of 'local administration' continues, as we shall see in the second part of the book.

CHAPTER 5

People in Local Government

1. THE ELECTED COUNCILLORS

Are elected councillors necessary?

THE question is posed bluntly, at the beginning of this chapter, for the simple reason that local authorities have existed for several years (at the time of writing) without any councillors, some simply being administered by a civil servant (a 'sole administrator'), others by a hand-picked committee of management. Times have been abnormal, with political upheaval and civil war, and it is perhaps unfair to try to answer the question against such a disturbed background. On the other hand sole administrators and committees of management were quite often appointed in earlier days, after some council had disgraced itself, and the evidence sometimes suggested that local administration worked better without elected councillors than with them.

It is clearly not *necessary* to have elected councillors in order to have efficient local administration. The theory is that they make local administration better by making it more representative—by turning it from local administration into local government; if they make it worse, as they frequently have done, it would be better to abolish them. The reason they have often made it worse is that a high proportion of them came into it solely for what they could extort through bribery and corruption, and of the rest few really understood their rôle, but interfered with their officials and dabbled in administration.

Assuming councillors to be on balance an advantage, it must be remembered that in most systems, e.g. the American, they leave most of the work, including all the administration, to professional hired staff, and concentrate on essentials. What are the essentials? They can be narrowed down to one word—priorities. Paid officials are more competent than elected councillors to do everything except represent the wishes of the people. This means that the hard core of the councillors' job is to decide whether people would rather remain as they are without being taxed, or be taxed and enjoy a better life; and if the latter, would they prefer a new school to a piped water supply, a feeder road to a maternity centre, a market to a tarred strip through the village to keep the dust down.

If this can be accepted, the rest of this chapter makes sense; if not, it is not worth the paper it is written on.

What is a local council?

A council, to use a customary legal description, is a 'body corporate, having perpetual succession and a common seal and having the power to sue and to be sued'. This means that the council is the local *authority*, upon which the Government lays certain powers and duties, which may tax people for local purposes, and which must accept responsibility for good government in such matters as are within its competence; it may also be disciplined by the higher authority of the Government if it misbehaves itself or is grossly negligent or inefficient. But the council consists of ordinary men and women elected by adult suffrage for a period of three years, and although their responsibility is corporate none of them can escape a measure of individual responsibility; each will discover this if he is, for example, a party to the misuse of the council's funds, since he may be 'surcharged', i.e. made to pay back from his own pocket his share of the money which has been misused.

Councillors, then, can be important people. British practice increases their importance by requiring them to meet frequently, to serve on many committees and subcommittees, and by giving them real, as distinct from nominal, responsibility in making plans and decisions. The staffs of local authorities, the local civil services so to speak, will carry on the routine business of the council without troubling the councillors; and principal officers may even make quite important decisions on their own authority; the extent to which they do this will depend very largely on personal relations and on local custom; but no principal officer will make a decision which involves a question of policy or principle, or the expenditure of public money, himself, but will always ask his committee for instructions. The ordinary councillor spends many hours a week on his work, and the chairman of a committee, particularly in a large authority, may find himself with practically a full-time job; for which, however, he is not paid anything.

It is not necessary for councillors to be worked so hard, or to have so much responsibility put upon them, or indeed to have so many councillors or so many committees. Local government in several other countries, although having a 'conciliar' system, asks far less of councillors and gives more responsibility to permanent officials; meetings are less frequent, committees are very much fewer and councils go into far less detail; even in neighbouring Eire this is so, for the local authorities there employ officials called 'managers', who, as their name implies, administer the affairs of the authority with a much freer hand than their British counterparts.

However, West Africa chose, rightly or wrongly, to follow British practice in this matter, and although many things changed since the early 1950s this particular aspect of local government did not.

It may as well be said bluntly, and at this early stage, that the quality and performance of councillors in West Africa was deeply disappointing. The system which was copied from Britain makes certain assumptions about councillors which it would be impossible to put into the law, but which are nevertheless more important than anything which *is* in the law; that is to say, the law governing this kind of local government can never work satisfactorily unless these assumptions are well founded.

One is that the men and women who offer themselves for election to local councils are people of some standing and reputation in their neighbourhood; from which it usually follows that they have established themselves in their own job or profession and do not stand for election with any idea of material profit for themselves. Another is that they are people of sufficient education or intelligence to be able to look at the problems of public welfare dispassionately, and to make decisions based on what they honestly think is best for the local community. Another is that whatever mixed motives may have caused them to become councillors, a dominant motive is that of public service. Another is that they are ordinarily honest.

There are some disadvantages in expecting these standards, the chief of which is that if councillors are to be people of some local standing and reputation they tend to be rather elderly, and it is generally thought that as people get older they become more conservative and less progressive. This tendency to be elderly is increased by the great demands that local government makes on councillors' time, since it is often only people who have retired, or are wealthy, or who are in the fortunate position of being their own masters, who can spare the necessary amount of time away from the job of earning their own living. This is particularly true of rural or scattered areas, where they have to travel some distance to attend meetings; it is less true in towns, where meetings are usually held in the evenings, after working hours.

But if assumptions of this kind are not made, local government may become valueless, or even dangerous.

The payment of councillors

This raises the whole question of the remuneration of councillors, and since there is no more thorny question in local government in West Africa it will be as well to deal with it now, before going on to discuss the normal duties of a councillor.

The first thing to be said is that the question of paying

certain councillors is one that has been discussed for some time in Britain and which may shortly have to be faced.[1] There is no question of *all* councillors in *all* kinds of councils being paid, for this would be unnecessary, intolerably expensive, and against public sentiment. Two things have happened, however, within recent years which makes the position of some leading councillors in the larger authorities (the county boroughs and the larger counties) increasingly burdensome. The first is that although these authorities have been losing some of their powers because some of their former functions have been 'nationalized', the total volume of their work has continued to grow, and they are now involved in vast development plans for education, health, public works and planning; the second is that social conditions have changed, in that there are fewer wealthy or leisured people than there used to be, and business and professional men have to give more and more time to their own occupations, and can no longer spare so much for public service. The burden on all councillors is considerable, but for those who are, for example, chairmen of important committees in the big authorities it is becoming intolerable. At some time in the near future local government may either have to pay such men or lose their services. The ordinary councillor is not in this position, but even so he is often not as fortunate as his predecessors in the early part of the century; moreover it is no longer acceptable to public opinion that service on councils should be the privilege of the few who, for whatever reason, are able to spare the time and the money, and local government is richer for the presence on its councils of ordinary wage-earners and housewives. It is interesting that less than twenty-five years ago there was no general code which allowed councillors even to claim their travelling or out-of-pocket expenses. Not until the Local Government Act of 1948 was this put on a systematic basis. This Act also

[1] Mayors of boroughs are normally given 'salaries' to enable them to perform their public and ceremonial duties, but this is not regarded as personal remuneration, and may well result in loss.

authorized, for the first time, payments to councillors to cover proved loss of earnings, though the great majority of councillors do not take advantage of this because their earnings cannot be shown to have diminished directly, though they may well have done so indirectly, as a result of their local government duties. All this reflects the fact that membership of local councils was normally regarded as a duty, a public service or a hobby, and the concessions that have been made are not intended to alter this principle.

But whereas in Britain the question of councillors' expenses was not dealt with for fifty years, and the actual payment of councillors has not even now been considered, in West Africa it has been a dominant consideration since the native authorities were first reorganized, and an extraordinary amount of public time has been consumed in discussing 'sitting allowances' (which are universally paid) and other forms of remuneration; while today there is a considerable demand for the actual payment of salaries. It would be wrong to criticize this solely in the light of British practice, for any such comparison would be superficial and misleading. The much more fundamental point is that councillors in the two countries are wholly different kinds of people; in other words, the 'assumptions' that we made a little earlier do not in fact apply in West Africa.

Past failures

Generally speaking, men who stand for local councils are not successful or established men; they are often very young, which is understandable since most of the older generation outside the towns would probably be illiterate; many of them are teachers, earning very small salaries; others have no definable occupation, and regard their council membership as a way of supplementing, if not actually earning, a living. A high proportion are neither intelligent nor honest, and it is these who deter more reputable citizens from standing for local councils. Above all, local councils have virtually become appendages of the political parties and the first qualification for a councillor was to be a political 'activist'. The dishonesty of councils has come to be taken for granted, a fact which can be stated openly since it is the subject of so many official reports. No one seriously questions the fact that the chief purpose of many—indeed most—councillors was to enrich themselves by percentages on contracts, bribes for favours and corrupt practice in general; or that nepotism, the giving of jobs, market stalls or contracts to relatives, was common practice.

All this is so familiar to West African readers that there is no point in dwelling on it. It is more profitable to point out that it constitutes a perversion, not an adaptation, of the British type of local government which was chosen in preference to any other. The system assumes conditions which do not exist in West Africa today. The questions which arise, constructively, are whether the position can be improved without the system being virtually destroyed; and what are, normally, the duties and responsibilities of councillors in this conciliar type of local government?

With regard to the first question, there has already been some improvement, and small though this may have been in relation to the problem as a whole it suggests that things are moving forward and not backward. It must be confessed that much of the improvement has been due to negative, or punitive, measures designed to prevent councillors from being corrupt and irresponsible. Thus it is now fairly common practice for 'the Minister', which in practice means a local administrative officer, to control the award of all contracts over a relatively small amount, to make or at least ratify all appointments to the staff above a certain level, and of course to scrutinize and approve a council's annual estimates. Moreover, the power of 'surcharge', that is the right of the Government to recover from individual councillors sums that have been improperly disbursed, is being more frequently used, specially in the Eastern Region of Nigeria; and this has had a salutary effect, as it makes councillors realize both that their responsibilities are serious and that the Government 'means business'.

Evidence of a more positive kind of improvement, arising from a growing sense of public service, is more difficult to give. All that can be given in fact is the hearsay evidence of people whose work is concerned with the local authorities and who have seen them at work over a number of years. What they have to say is sometimes mildly encouraging, at other times pessimistic. It can be said as a fact that expenditure by and through local authorities has grown steadily in the twenty years between the early 1950s and the early 1970s, that despite many amendments to the law the main fabric of the new local authorities has been preserved, even though towards the end of the 1960s elected councillors were dismissed and superseded by nominated 'committees of management' or 'sole administrators'. In part they brought their dismissal upon themselves, for the reasons we have just discussed; in part they were the victims of partisan, and increasingly violent, politics. But without the framework of local authorities, whoever was in charge of them, the central departments of government would have been intolerably hard pressed. But at the personal level—and we are discussing councillors, who are supposed to be the living embodiment of local government—there was little evidence that men of higher calibre were seeking election, that a spirit of public service was growing or that bribery, corruption and nepotism were in decline.

The reasons for this are complex, and beyond the scope of this book, but the principal ones must just be mentioned, even if there is no space to elaborate them. First, local government is an alien institution which does not yet command much loyalty; men who are completely honest in their dealings with family, clan and tribe or any indigenous institution are often dishonest in their dealings as councillors. Second, the total number of people available in West Africa of the kind which the British type of local government takes for granted is small; such as they are, they are much more drawn to national politics or to their professions and businesses than to the rather trivial and often sordid affairs of local councils. Third, and arising from the second, the majority of people engaging in rural local government must necessarily, at this stage, be illiterate, and it is not easy for men of higher calibre to work alongside them; in any case such men usually gravitate to the towns. Fourth, the council areas are small in population and revenue, and the volume and importance of the business each is able to handle is such that men of standing are not interested in it. Fifth, as we have said, the councils are so deeply embroiled in politics that busy people with businesses or professions of their own cannot be bothered with them; or alternatively if they have political interests they are in national, not local, politics.

None of these considerations ought to apply in the large towns, where the work of the councils is sufficiently challenging to tax the powers of the most able, where the revenues, though inadequate, are at least sufficient to bring about visible improvements, and where there is a sufficient concentration of educated and established citizens to satisfy the demands of the British type of local government. It must be confessed, however, that their record is no better than that of the rural councils; in Nigeria alone, all the major urban authorities, Lagos, Abeokuta, Ibadan, Kano, Onitsha, Enugu, Aba and Port Harcourt were the subject of official enquiries into maladministration and corruption long before the suspension of elected councils.

The second question—whether the system can be sufficiently improved without destroying it—is one that can only be answered as the book proceeds. Already a number of the undoubted improvements, such as the closer control of councils by the central government, are a contradiction of the kind of local government which was first envisaged, which depends on having as much, not as little, local autonomy as possible. However, we said in the first chapter that we were studying a foreign system which was in the process of adapting itself to local circumstances, and we must not be surprised if some of these adaptations are of a radical kind.

Having considered what sort of people local councillors

are supposed to be, let us consider how they come to be elected and what they are supposed to do.

The election of councillors

In the first place they are elected to represent a small 'constituency', often called a 'ward'. Usually they attain their office by direct election, and the procedure hardly differs from that of a parliamentary election. In Western Nigeria of the 1960s not all council members were elected, as a proportion of places was reserved for 'traditional' members, that is chiefs and their office holders; this was so also in Ghana until 1961, when the Government adopted a new principle whereby chiefs were excluded from local councils, but in compensation for this traditional councils were given new status under the Chieftaincy Act 1961. The whole question of traditional elements in local government will be discussed later in the chapter.[2]

But although direct election has been normal there have been instances of *indirect* election also, that is election from a lower council to a higher one. This is the oldest pattern of elections in Africa and in general it has fallen into disfavour as being 'undemocratic'. In theory this is not strictly true—one pattern is not necessarily either more or less democratic than the other. It *is* true on the other hand that in developing countries indirect elections are liable to favour age and conservatism, since the primary 'electoral college', which might be a council of village elders, will reflect its outlook in the one above it. On the other hand if the lowest electoral college is itself elected this bias ought to be removed, or at least diminished, and certainly in Western Nigeria, which was progressive in its political thinking, divisional councillors were elected by the constituent district councils, and not by the electors, as late as the mid-1960s. Moreover the new Ghanaian Constitution,

[2] It is impossible for reasons of space to refer to Northern Nigeria in this context, for there, in the 1950s and 1960s, there was every variety of council membership, from Chief-in-Council to full election. The facts are summarized in chapter 11.

and the Local Administration Act of 1971, reintroduces the indirect principle in elections from District to Regional Councils.

Each method has its advocates, and it will be interesting to see whether there is a return to favour of the indirect method, which has two very great advantages—it costs nothing whereas direct elections cost a great deal; and it ensures a systematic chain of representation.

The duties of councillors

The first duty of a councillor is to represent the people who elected him, and here a curious misunderstanding often arises. So strong is local rivalry, of a quasi-political kind, that many councillors (and even some MPs) appear to think that they represent only the people who voted for them—their own supporters. If it is suggested that they equally represent the people who voted against them, provided they live in the same ward, they are surprised; if it is then asked *who* represents these people, the answer is that they have no representative because they voted for the losing candidate. This raises an important question of principle in representative democracy, and introduces the difference between a 'representative' and a 'delegate'. The theory of this kind of democracy is that a man represents all the people who live in a certain area, whether they voted for him or not, or whether they voted at all; his concern is with the total welfare of that constituency or ward. Moreover he has, in theory at any rate, the full right to speak and vote according to his own judgment, and is not tied down by what 'his people' have told him to say, or expect him to say; this happens more rarely than it used to, in Britain as elsewhere, because councillors are increasingly elected with the help of political parties, and are expected to conform to the policies of these parties; but the principle remains, and from time to time a man takes an individual and unpopular line, but nevertheless cannot be removed from his seat on the council, or in Parliament, until the next election.

Furthermore, if a man may only speak and vote in the way he has been instructed by his supporters, he is a 'delegate' or mouthpiece, and not a 'representative'. Democracy of this kind is quite legitimate, and if West Africa prefers it there is no reason to feel ashamed of it; but it is different from representative democracy, and it has the disadvantage that a man's constituents who are not also his personal supporters are virtually disfranchised.

The theory really goes a little further than this. A councillor (or MP) is supposed to think of the welfare of his local authority (or country) and not primarily of his ward (or constituency). While it is of course legitimate for him to press the interests of his own ward he should be willing to subordinate them to the interests of his council area as a whole. But this is an attitude which requires a great deal of restraint and maturity, and it is significant that there have been complaints in the West African Press that when Parliament assembles Members do little more than press the Government to provide amenities in their own constituencies.

The councillor's second duty is to attend meetings. This book is intended to promote thought and discussion, and is not a handbook for councillors, or a manual of the procedure governing meetings; accordingly little space will be given to such questions as standing orders, debating procedure, the tabling of motions or the conduct of day-to-day business. It may be doubted whether these are in any case matters of first importance at this stage; it is possible that too much emphasis has been placed upon them in the past, since in practice councils either conduct their business with great informality, or, if they attempt to follow complicated foreign rules and conventions of procedure they become so involved in them that it becomes impossible for any business to proceed at all. This is one of the many matters in which West Africans would be better advised to follow their own instincts and modes of behaviour instead of relying on British practice. Nevertheless, meetings anywhere would be chaotic if they were not governed by rules, and it is the councillor's responsibility to understand them and abide by them; they govern such matters as the order of business, how he may introduce a matter to his council, how long and how often he may speak, how subjects are brought to a conclusion, how voting takes place and how decisions are implemented. He is also expected to study his agenda papers and give some thought to the business before the meeting takes place; sometimes this is all too easy, as the agenda is brief and uninformative, but a well-prepared agenda will include a great deal of information, prepared by the council's officials, and consisting largely of the reports of committees, which set out the facts, the problems and the alternative courses of action open to the council in making its decisions. It follows from what has been said in this paragraph that the lot of the illiterate or uneducated councillor is not an easy one; indeed it is questionable whether this kind of local government should be operated at all by councillors below a certain level of education.

The committee system

Under the system that has been adopted in West Africa the councils work very largely through committees, a habit for which the British are specially renowned. It is now accepted in Britain, however, that committees, though important, have been greatly overdone, and the present tendency is to reduce their number by grouping them together under a few main heads, e.g. social services, engineering and works, finance, etc.

Committees are obviously necessary. A council cannot consider its estimates unless they have been prepared in advance; it cannot decide whether to build a school unless someone has gone into such matters as siting, design and cost; it cannot employ a member of staff unless a few people have interviewed the most likely candidates. Unless, therefore, the preparation of business is to be left to the council's permanent staff, which is the other alternative, a council's business must be very largely done in committee, and this is in fact where most of the important work is done in British local government. The power of delegation is fairly widely used in Britain, and the council, in full session, accepts or ratifies the vast majority of its committees' decisions without question, only debating particularly contentious matters of points of principle.

What went wrong in the past, and what is now being rectified, was that councils continually appointed new committees with narrow jurisdictions instead of widening the jurisdiction of existing ones.

The committee system only works satisfactorily if certain conventions (i.e. unwritten rules) are observed. One is that when committees are appointed they shall be representative of all points of view, and not narrowly sectional. This has not always been done in West Africa, and it is significant that in Western Nigeria a section was included in the law giving the Minister the right to require a council to appoint certain other members if he thinks that the committee in question had been 'packed'; in plain language, if the ruling party had put all its supporters on the committee and none of its opponents. Another is that the council shall not do the work of its committees all over again in full session, a temptation into which many West African councils fell; even if a committee has not been given delegated powers, and if its conclusions are therefore subject to the approval of the council, it is a waste of time and energy, and a denial of the committee system, to go over the whole ground again instead of debating and deciding the vital point.

A local Parliament?

It is sometimes asked whether a local government council is a sort of miniature Parliament, a question to which there are two different answers in West Africa. The essence of Parliament in this context is that there should be a number of leading members (i.e. elected representatives), charged with important policy-making and administrative responsibilities as Ministers, and with a staff of civil servants. Such a pattern is in fact to be found in the Northern States of Nigeria, where 'executive councillors' may be responsible for particular departments of the council's work, e.g. public works, agriculture and forestry, education, health or personnel. The original reason for this may have been that the shortage of educated men made it difficult to staff the 'native authorities' with men who could perform their duties without supervision, but there is no reason why the system should not be considered strictly on its merits, as long as it is remembered that the 'NAS' in question were large in terms of finance and population, and that departmental work was possible; the executive councillor system would make no sense in the smaller councils elsewhere. In a rather less precise way local councils in some other parts of Africa have resembled tribal parliaments—the chiefdom councils of Sierra Leone are an example on a small scale, but bigger examples can be seen in parts of East and Central Africa.

On the other hand in the 'western' system which was adopted in southern Nigeria and Ghana, no local councillor has any administrative responsibility whatever. This even applies to the mayor of a municipality; he has certain privileges and prestige as the town's chief citizen, and has certain civic duties to discharge which no other councillor can discharge; but even he is just an ordinary councillor as far as executive responsibility is concerned. It is the staff, and not the councillors, who implement the decisions made by the council; and it is the responsibility of the chief executive officer, the secretary, to see that they are implemented. The distinction between the legislative function of the councillor and the executive function of the staff has often been blurred in West Africa, with the result that councillors have interfered in the work of the secretary's office, written letters on behalf of the council, and given instructions to members of the staff. This is contrary to the intention of the local government laws and to the accepted practice of this particular type of local democracy.

Traditional members of councils

The form of local government which preceded the present one was known as native administration. It lasted in Eastern Nigeria until 1950, in Ghana until 1951 and in Western Nigeria until 1952. In Ghana and Western Nigeria it was founded on the institution of chieftainship, and what we would now think of as the local council was the chief and his traditional office bearers and advisers. No member was elected through the ballot box.

When elected councils were introduced the position of the chief was seriously affected. Was he to be superseded by the elected council? Was he to preside over it? Was his voice to count for no more than anybody else's voice? These were difficult questions. On the one hand it could be argued that the chiefs, or most of them, were old men, were illiterate, had been brought up in a tradition that was passing away, and knew little or nothing of the working of a modern institution designed to develop social services. On the other hand it could be said with equal truth that the great majority of people retained—indeed still retain—a respect for the chiefs, that they were the accepted source of authority in all customary matters, and that to leave the chief out of the government of his locality was unthinkable. Moreover, although the numerical majority of the chiefs may have been simple and illiterate men there were many outstanding exceptions; several paramount chiefs and obas were educated and progressive men with a notable record of public service in national affairs.

The problem was tackled by a compromise. Councils were to be elected, but a minority of seats was to be reserved for chiefs and other 'traditional' members, and usually the chief became the ceremonial president, as distinct from the working chairman, of the new councils. In the Western Region of Nigeria the law was that 'the Instrument relating to a council shall include traditional members', without specifying any maximum, a change from the original fixed proportion. Eastern Nigeria was not originally concerned in this matter, but in 1960 their

Government decided that 'all first and second class chiefs should be appointed traditional members of their respective county councils, and the Instruments of these councils were amended to provide for these appointments'.[3]

These arrangements have been much criticized, on three grounds. First, that the significance of chieftainship is largely removed if chiefs or traditional members can be outvoted by elected members, especially by young and sometimes irresponsible men; certainly the traditional members themselves have often complained of this. Second, that the traditional members are often not really interested in the modern affairs of the councils, and are a drag on the wheels because they constantly intrigue for the maintenance of their own local power and prestige. Third (in Nigeria), because governments have used their power to nominate traditional members as a device to get support for their own parties and policies.

Taken together, these criticisms carry considerable weight, and no doubt they were in the mind of the Government of Ghana when, in 1961, the Government settled the argument by taking the chiefs out of local government altogether, but regularizing their position in a Chieftaincy Act which established their own traditional councils for traditional purposes. For many years chieftaincy disputes, or quarrels between the traditional and elected elements, had laid a tremendous burden on the Ministry of Local Government, and the work involved was unrewarding and unconstructive.

Since it is difficult to argue that the purposes of local government, as set out in Acts of Parliament, have very much to do with traditional matters such as titles, customary law, inheritance or matrimonial affairs, it certainly seems logical to separate them in this way. On the other hand the institution of chieftainship is not something that will just die out in the course of a generation, and for the time being the chief may be a key figure not only in tradi-

[3] Annual Report of the Ministry of Local Government, 1960–61.

tion and ceremony but in modern affairs. For example, there are many areas where, if the Government wants something to be made known, about a census for instance, or a disease of crops or cattle, the most efficient channel of communication will be the chief. Or again, effective community development may depend upon his leadership. It is interesting to note that ten years after the Ghanaian chiefs were dismissed from local government they and their entourages were restored to it in the Local Administration Act 1971 by being given up to a third of the seats on District Councils and up to a half on Local Councils, whose main purpose was to be community development. It is difficult to generalize when there are so many shades of difference in the nature of society—and in the chiefs themselves. This must remain for some time one of the unsolved problems of local government in West Africa.

Some Africans have observed that there is a British precedent for including a proportion of traditional members on certain councils, because of the office of 'alderman', which might roughly be translated 'elder' if not 'chief'! But the argument does not stand examination. It is true that the office of alderman is a departure from direct representative democracy, and many people in Britain criticize it on that ground; indeed, proposals are made from time to time to do away with it.

It originated in the Municipal Corporations Act of 1835, when borough councils were first elected on a systematic ratepayers' franchise and was, to put it bluntly, a concession to Conservative fears that fully elected councils would not be fit to govern properly; a sentiment with which Africans will be familiar from colonial days, and which it is interesting to find in nineteenth-century Britain. The principle, which was later extended to county councils, ensures that a quarter of the council members are elected, not by the electorate, but by the council itself, either from inside or outside its own membership; moveover such members hold office for six years instead of three. During the 130 years that have passed the real reason for its institution has tended to be forgotten, and it is now rationalized on the ground that it provides additional stability and experience, and may be used either to gain the services of some exceptionally able person, or to reward long and faithful service. It has indeed been used to good effect for both purposes, and in councils governed by party politics there has generally been some sensible agreement between the parties for the distribution of aldermanic seats. Of recent years, however, it has also been abused by political parties, who have been known to use their electoral powers, in evenly balanced councils, to maintain their own majority.

It is a debatable matter. The immediate point is that it can hardly be compared accurately with the institution of chieftainship in Africa; indeed, in the African context one can rather imagine it being quoted as a neo-colonialist device.

2. THE FULL-TIME STAFF

Although responsibility for the acts and decisions of a local authority rests with the elected council, the actual work must be carried out by its paid staff. The staff are not altogether free from some personal responsibility themselves; it is their duty to advise their council and loyally to implement the council's policy; on the other hand, if they believe that any decision of the council is improper they have a right to have their opinion recorded, while if they believe it to be illegal they have a direct duty to the public and the Government to refuse to implement it. But leaving aside such unlikely possibilities it is broadly true to say that the elected councillors arrive at decisions and that the staff translate these decisions into action. How does this work in practice? Once more it will be useful to see how it works in Britain, from which the system derived, and then to see what departures from British practice have been made in recent years in response to local circumstances; they are in fact considerable.

Britain and West Africa compared

It must first be emphasized that no realistic comparison can be drawn between the staffs of British local authorities and those in the parts of West Africa which we are discussing. The staff of a major British authority, urban or rural, will include numbers of men and women with professional and technical qualifications in the fields of engineering, medicine, public health, education, accountancy and law; and even a small urban or rural district will employ a professionally qualified secretary, treasurer, engineer, surveyor, medical officer and sanitary inspector; in Southern Nigeria and Ghana the corresponding people are in central, not local government employment. For the most part the local authorities in West Africa are staffed by a secretary, a treasurer (though often these two posts are combined) and a works foreman or supervisor with little mechanical equipment and only a small staff of unskilled labourers; even the big cities have a staff equivalent, at most, to an English rural district council; there may also, according to local policy in this matter, be a local education officer. This situation arises partly from the different share in national administration which is borne by local authorities in the two places, partly from the small financial scale on which West African local authorities operate, and partly from the chronic shortage of qualified staff in the professional and technical ranges.

In Britain these local officials, together with their subordinate and clerical staffs, are engaged and paid by the local authorities, and are in the fullest sense their employees; if they wish to change their job, from one authority to another, they must apply for a post in answer to an advertisement, as there is no central direction in matters of this kind. Service in local government, covering a very wide range of occupations, is regarded as an honourable profession in itself, and the principal officers have a status as high as the most senior civil servants. There is, to be precise, a certain amount of central control over a few professional appointments; medical officers of health and sanitary inspectors are protected from dismissal by the Minister, and their duties and qualifications may also be prescribed by him; also chief constables and chief education officers may only be appointed with the approval of the Home Secretary or the Minister of Education; there are very good reasons for these particular controls, but they are exceptions to the general rule, and all the officials concerned are employees of the local authority, and not of the Government, even though the Government reserves the right to have a say in their appointment or dismissal.

Service in local government, then, is a profession which embraces many other professions; the wider professional interest is safeguarded through a national association or trade union, the National and Local Government Officers' Association (NALGO), besides which there are many 'internal' professional associations, such as those of town clerks, municipal engineers, municipal treasurers, public health officers and so on. These are of course voluntary associations and have nothing to do either with the central departments or the local authorities.

These local authority staffs, numbering thousands in a large authority and hundreds even in a medium-sized one, are, so to speak, the elected council's 'civil service', and enjoy the same respect and the same neutrality as the actual Civil Service. The principal officers are expected to advise the council, or more particularly the committee responsible for their own field of work, and when a committee or council decision has been made they are expected to implement it loyally, whether they agree with it or not. In practice, sharp disagreement rarely arises, because of the conventions which have grown up about the relationship of councillors and officials. It is always difficult to describe a convention, which is simply an accepted code of behaviour, though a convention may often be as important as a law. In this instance the key to the relationship is mutual respect. Constitutionally the council is the master and the official is its servant; conventionally, they work as partners in a team; what results from this is usually a workable compromise between what the expert would like and what the layman considers possible.

Since this relationship is the vital core of local government, and since it has lamentably failed to establish itself in West Africa, it is worth dwelling on it for another moment. Many West African observers in Britain have come to the conclusion that local government is a sham, because everything of any importance appears to them to be settled by the officials, who merely pull the councillors along with them. This is partly a surprised reaction from the situation in West Africa itself, where councillors tend to 'throw their weight about' and treat their officials as subordinate; and partly a misunderstanding of the relationship they observe in England. Officials who have worked for a council for a long time, and have demonstrated their efficiency and loyalty, are naturally entrusted with very large responsibilities; they are, after all, professional men, highly qualified and highly paid, and local government is their career; no sensible body of councillors will want to diminish their responsibilities or to 'cramp their style'. They are experts in their subject, they spend their whole time on it, and they know far more about it than the council. What the council, or its committees, is concerned with, is that the official shall keep in close touch with his chairman, that matters of policy shall be decided by elected representatives and not by officials, and that plans of development shall be submitted to them, with full information about the pros and cons of alternative courses, so that they may decide what is best in the interest of their fellow citizens. It must be remembered, however, that all the information and expert knowledge, as well as most of the initiative and imagination, come from the official, whose job it is to supply them; they do not come from the councillors. The job of the elected representative is to examine the officials' plans in the light of what money is available, what course of action will commend itself to the electors whom they represent, what can be done now and what must

be postponed, and, occasionally, whether the professional
expert in his enthusiasm is wanting to go further than public
opinion will allow. The councillors, after all, are experts
in one thing only—judging the wishes of the ratepayers
and electors, and using their own common sense about
what ought to be done.

Accordingly, if the relationship is good the councillors
will give their officials a very free hand to get on with their
professional job; and the officials for their part will be
careful not to abuse this privilege by taking decisions about
which their 'masters' might want to express an opinion.
Since this mutual confidence generally exists, local government on the British pattern works; if it did not exist, it
would be better to try some other system altogether. But
it exists only because councillors are sensible people, and
officials are competent and conscientious.

Finally, with regard to Britain, officials are completely
outside the party political battle. Like civil servants, they
serve a Labour or Conservative council with equal fidelity;
and no councillor would know, or would be interested in,
the personal political beliefs of the council's employees.
Local government employees have in fact somewhat wider
freedom to take part in politics than most civil servants,
but senior officials of a local authority would certainly not
take advantage of this, and would confine their politics to
using their vote every few years.

This is the kind of situation which the Local Government
Ordinances in West Africa sought to reproduce. They
failed, almost completely. Let us take the points one by
one and consider why they failed, and what pattern took
their place.

West Africa—The Employer
First, the employment of staff by local authorities, acting
as independent employers, gradually gave way to control
or even employment by the Government, thus creating a
centralized or 'unified' local government service. This was

found necessary in order to protect local government staff from being victimized by irresponsible employing councils. The earlier local government Ordinances aimed at reproducing the British situation, but it was found that when councils were given this independent status as employers they frequently abused it; thus men who were performing their duties satisfactorily were dismissed because they did not belong to the right political party, or faction, or family, and were replaced by favourite sons of the party or by relatives of influential councillors. Apart from being unjust this was completely demoralizing for the staffs of local authorities everywhere, and it would have become impossible to hold anyone in local government service, let alone attract men of a higher calibre, if governments had not assumed a large measure of control. Another complication, not necessarily involving corruption, was that councils which had a free hand in the appointment of their more senior employees would frequently appoint a local man, a 'son of the soil', in preference to a better qualified man from elsewhere. It could of course be argued that, other things being equal, a son of the soil might give better service to his council than a 'stranger', but even in the best circumstances the method has its disadvantages. First, sons of the soil were too deeply involved in local politics, feuds and personalities to stand any chance of being impartial; and second, it was a method which blocked that free movement from one place to another, by which senior local government officers normally gain both their experience and promotion. Accordingly, governments have, in varying degrees, stepped in both to protect and to control the employees of local authorities.

The first of all the local government ordinances—the Eastern Region (of Nigeria) Ordinance of 1950—gave councils a free hand in the appointment of staff who were paid less than £400 a year; above that figure the authority of the Government was required, but in all cases the local authority could itself determine what was a reasonable remuneration for the various posts. This freedom was severely restricted in the subsequent Ordinance of 1955, which decreed that the appointment of *all* staff (even including daily-paid labourers) must be subject to the approval of the Minister, and that *no* employee was to be dismissed for any reason without the Minister's written approval; moreover the Minister assumed power to determine, if he thought fit, what was reasonable remuneration for any given post. Later the Minister did in fact lay down comprehensive regulations governing the whole field of appointments to local authority staff, including salaries, grades of employment, qualifications, procedure to be followed in making appointments, and discipline. These were long strides in the direction of central control, but an even more significant change was made in 1958, when the Minister assumed power to 'transfer an officer or member of the staff of a council to the service of another council within the Region'. Since that date many hundreds of such transfers were in fact made, with a mixture of happy and unhappy results; happy, in that the air was cleared, more men were given appropriate responsibilities and escaped from the deadening prospect of life-long employment with one small council (the curse of the 'son of the soil' policy), and corruption was diminished; unhappy, in that the number of transfers was excessive, to the point of having a generally unsettling effect, that men simply moved from one set of local entanglements to another, and as a result constantly moved from place to place. It is one thing for the Minister to decree that a man shall serve in a given place, but if local government is to mean anything at all he can only do so fruitfully if he is acceptable to a local council and if they make his path easy.

It is strange that having gone so far towards central control the Government did not take the final step (as it did in the Western Region) of formally establishing a unified local government service. It stopped just short of this. There was a Local Government Service Board, but its powers were advisory and not executive; and the councils still had the power to recommend the original appointments, either as a result of advertising for candidates or by choosing someone they want to employ.

The Western Region approached the matter a little differently. It created a Unified Local Government Service in the formal sense, and established a Local Government Service Board with executive, as distinct from advisory, powers. On the other hand it did not bring *all* local council employees within the scope either of the Service or the Board, but only those who were deemed to hold 'superior posts'; the definition of a superior post was made by the Governor in Council, and could be extended from time to time.

The Ghana Local Government Act of 1961 reached the same destination by a slightly different route. In principle, it left all councils free to appoint and dismiss their own staff, and thus held to the original intention inherited from British practice. But this was subject to a vitally important qualification, contained in section 125 of the Act, which allowed the Minister, *with the prior approval of the President*, to make staff regulations covering every detail of employment—qualifications, pay, promotion, discipline and 'terms and conditions of service generally'; moreover these regulations could apply to 'any class or grade of officer' in local government employment. The section also established a 'Local Government Central Advisory Committee' whose functions could in turn be delegated to regional committees. It thus made possible a complete apparatus of central control over local government staff, and one moreover of which the President was the ultimate head.

Another section gave the Minister a further significant power:

'. . . a council may, with the approval of the Minister and with the consent of the officer concerned, *and shall if the Minister so directs*, appoint to any office in its service a person who is a public officer seconded to the service of the council for that purpose. . . .'

In other words, administrative officers of the central

government could be seconded as local government officials. The Southern Nigerian laws included a somewhat similar, but less positive, provision; there a council could appoint such an officer if the Governor or Minister approved, but the Minister did not assume the original power himself. The secondment of administrative officers to certain councils, and for particular reasons, could be a useful device, and was at one time favoured in Western Nigeria. Its obvious limitation was that there were many councils and few administrative officers, who are greatly in demand for other duties. Accordingly it could only be used in very exceptional circumstances, and Western Nigeria was never able to develop it, although it had some success.

Thus, the details differed, but the general trend was the same—a trend away from the full independence of councils in appointing staff, and towards supervision by the central authority. Whether this trend was healthy or unhealthy must remain a matter of opinion, and the fact was that the arguments were very evenly balanced. On the one hand those accustomed to the British approach would argue that independence in the appointment of staff (with the professional exceptions already referred to) is absolutely basic to the whole concept of local government; that a so-called unified local government service is simply a junior civil service, a poor relation of the proper one; that it would be more logical to 'go the whole hog' and incorporate local government officers in the real Civil Service; and that then the local authorities would have become mere agents or organs of the central government. They object also to the Minister, a politician, having overriding powers in such an intimate and vital matter, since it lays the whole local government structure open to political influence, and may affect the freedom of local councils to be of a different political complexion from the Government. Others will argue that this is a counsel of perfection; that corruption, nepotism and 'sons of the soil' are a brake on progress and efficiency and must be strictly controlled until their influence in West African public life diminishes; and that this control may be regarded as a temporary expedient until West African politics and administration develop greater maturity and impartiality. This is not the place to give a final judgment; our purpose is simply to record a departure from the original intention, and the reasons for it.

West Africa—The councillor-staff relationship

Second, a good working relationship between councillors and staff has rarely been established. Instead of being based on mutual respect and equal partnership it has tended to be a master-servant relationship, based on attempted domination by councillors. This is understandable, but it is necessary to consider the reasons for it.

The true relationship between councillors and officials was never elaborated in the law of local government either in Britain or West Africa, and it would in fact be impossible to define it legally. It is one of those things which is essentially governed by convention rather than by statute, and conventions grow out of local circumstances. It would be absurd to expect the same conventions to grow out of the very different circumstances of West Africa and Britain.

The principal officers of a British local authority are men of high professional standing; as a broad generalization they are probably better educated, better qualified and better paid than many of the councillors whose servants they technically are. Councillors for their part are men and women busy with their own affairs, to whom local government is voluntary public service, and who think too highly of the ability of their officials to want to interfere with them or try to dominate them. Out of these circumstances grows the delicately balanced relationship of working partners, each recognizing the other's authority in their respective spheres.

The principal officers of most West African local authorities are few in number, their professional qualifications are very modest, and they are not highly paid in comparison with civil servants. A high proportion of West

African local councillors, on the other hand, were not people of high attainments, many of them were in local government for material gain, and they had little respect for their officials. Out of these circumstances it was natural that there should have grown a different relationship.

This is certainly a case where convention is more important than law, for if a legal definition of the relationship is insisted on it can only be that the council is the master and the officials are its servants, since the council is the statutory authority and the officials (with the reservations we have mentioned) are its employees and agents. But the kind of local government which West Africa has inherited from British tradition will not work on these lines. It results in inefficiency and corruption on the one hand and the continual frustration of officials on the other. This was perhaps the worst miscalculation in importing an alien political institution from Britain. It was easy to import the outward forms, as expressed in legislation, but impossible to import the spirit and the conventions which have taken a long time to grow, and which are the only reason why legislation of this type has proved workable. A narrowly legalistic interpretation can only tend towards domination by councillors who are not fit to dominate, and in circumstances where domination is in any case out of place.

Finally, we come to party politics, a subject which is discussed more fully in the next chapter. Here it is sufficient to say that local government in West Africa became so closely meshed with politics that it was virtually impossible for an official to enjoy the neutrality of the his British counterpart. The personal political allegiance of officials was a matter of great interest to the councillors of the majority party; many competent officials fell by the wayside because their political allegiance was the wrong one, and many others had to 'toe a party line' in order to survive and do their work. This was a development which had not been anticipated when the first Local Government Ordinances were passed in the early 1950s, but it quickly became apparent and is now taken for granted. It is another fundamental departure from British practice.

The work of the staff

So much for the background against which the staffs of local authorities are intended to do their work. The actual nature of this work could only be described satisfactorily in a handbook, or a working manual, and such a description would be out of place in a general survey of this kind; in any case the standing orders and regulations which govern the day-to-day work of officials vary from country to country, and from small rural authorities to large urban ones. Accordingly we will only attempt a few general remarks.

In Britain the chief executive officer is usually described by the old-fashioned title of clerk to the council, but in West Africa the simple word secretary is preferred. The secretary is the general purpose man, who is responsible first for the meetings of the council and its committees; second for the internal organization of the council offices; and third for the council's dealings with the public and the Government. In the first of these capacities he must summon meetings, prepare the agenda and reports, keep the minutes and other records, and implement the council's decisions; in the second he is responsible for office organization, delegation and co-ordination of work, staff matters and discipline; in his final capacity he negotiates with the Ministry of Local Government, writes the council's letters, conducts interviews on their behalf, deals with contracts and listens to members of the general public. In a small council he will do all this himself, but in larger councils he will have to practise the real art of the administrator, which is delegation; that is to say, another member of his staff may be placed in charge of the work of certain committees, another may be made wholly responsible for minutes and records, another for interviewing members of the public and so on. This kind of delegation grows as the size of the council grows, and in large municipal councils like

Freetown, Accra and Lagos the internal organization will become quite elaborate. The basic qualification for the clerk to a council in Britain is that of a solicitor, since he must be familiar with a considerable body of law and must be competent to advise his council upon it. Few secretaries in West Africa outside the big cities have a legal qualification, since neither the responsibilities nor the salaries in local government are yet sufficient to attract such men, but they must nevertheless have a working knowledge not only of the law of local government but of a wide range of Acts or Ordinances which impinge on the work of a local authority. The duties of a secretary are varied, responsible and interesting, and if the authorities were larger in size and financial resources, and if secretaries were able to work free from the interference of councillors or the entanglement of politics, it would be a profession that should attract men of high educational and professional qualifications. But for reasons which we have discussed it is still struggling for prestige, and only in the big cities does it have the status which it deserves, and which it enjoys in more developed countries.

These general remarks apply also to the treasurer, whose responsibilities are narrower but equally onerous; indeed, he usually controls a larger number of subordinate staff because of the continual routine work of revenue collecting, receipting, making and checking of payments, safeguarding of cash and bringing receipts and payments to account. There has been a great deal of financial fraud in local government treasuries, but seen in perspective, and remembering their small salaries and lack of training, treasurers and their staffs deserve a good deal of credit for what they have managed to achieve. Their work, for the most part, is made easier by the fact that government treasuries still insist that they shall follow detailed financial instructions and memoranda, so that the form of their estimates, income and expediture accounts and balance sheets are closely prescribed, partly in order to assist those who are unskilled in accounting methods and partly to prevent or minimize the possibility of fraud. The treasurer must be thoroughly familiar with these regulations, must be able to advise his council on financial matters, and may have to be prepared to oppose it if he considers its financial decisions unwise or improper; unfortunately this is a situation which arises only too often.

The secretary and treasurer, with the assistants and subordinate staff, comprise the administration; but while no local authority could work without efficient administration, it would be equally true to say that local government would be pointless if it consisted of efficient administration alone. An administration which produced nothing in terms of the welfare of the public would be useless, however internally efficient. Here we come to the current weakness of West African local government, which is its lack of other professional and technical officers. We referred on page 53 to the immense variety of functions which councils may by law perform, and to the contrast with the narrow range of functions which they do in fact perform because of their lack of qualified staff.

The two basic skills needed in local government are in engineering and public health; but apart from the largest urban authorities, who may employ their own engineer and medical officer, it usually falls to the central government to supply professional knowledge and advice. That is to say a provincial engineer or medical officer will give his services to the local authorities within his area, in addition to carrying out his central responsibilities. In Ghana, a notable attempt was made to make good the technical deficiencies of local authorities by setting up in three of the eight regions 'Technical Advice Centres', staffed by qualified engineers and architects. Within the local authority itself the highest qualified officer would probably be a works supervisor, assisted by a few artisans such as carpenters, plumbers and motor mechanics, but otherwise only be labourers; or in the field of public health a sanitary or health inspector, a midwife and a dispensary assistant.

Local education officers and teachers may also be in a

council's employ, but this depends on the division of labour in education between the central and local authorities, usually in the field of primary education. In a sense *all* the work of local authorities turns on this division of labour. The point for the moment is that local authorities are expected to be able to provide, largely out of their own resources but with varying degrees of financial grant aid, the staff necessary for their own administration and for minor public works and public health services.

One final matter which may be touched on in conclusion is the right of local government officials to combine in their own interest through trade union action. The profession of local government in Britain owes much of its status, and officials owe their regular salary scales and conditions of service, to the work of NALGO over sixty years; though it is fair to add that NALGO has always been as insistent on high professional ethical standards as on bargaining for the welfare of its members. We have already seen that the entry of governments into this field, through unified local government services, has to some extent made such activity unnecessary. Nevertheless, attempts have been made in West Africa to form staff associations of various kinds, though like most trade unions they have suffered from poor organization, an unwillingness on the part of members to pay subscriptions, and consequently a weak bargaining position. More successful efforts have been made of recent years to form 'Associations of Local Authorities', which are not quite the same thing as trade unions. They really stand for the interests of local authorities as such, rather than for the welfare of employees. Their function in Britain, where they exist under such names as the Association of Municipal Corporations and the County Councils Association, is to protect the rights and further the interests of local authorities, or of particular kinds of local authorities. It is very largely a parliamentary one— that is to say they keep a careful watch on all legislation which will directly or indirectly affect local authorities, and make representations on appropriate matters to Ministers or departmental officials; further, they have established a position of trust and confidence whereby the Government frequently consults them on local government affairs when legislation is being contemplated or drafted. This is extremely important work, but it is not trade union work, and members of these associations include councillors and officials alike. An association of local authorities, originating in Western Nigeria but spreading to other parts of English-speaking West Africa, is in a sense attempting to combine both functions.

Over the last ten years local government in West Africa has grown visibly in importance, judged solely by the amount of public money which is channelled through it; it has not grown correspondingly in stature and prestige, or established itself as a profession comparable in importance with the Civil Service. A responsible professional association or trade union could be one of the main instruments in remedying this situation.

CHAPTER 6

Party Politics in Local Government

(NOTE: At the time of writing there are no party politics in the Federation of Nigeria; in the past, however, they have dominated local government, and in large measure contributed to its failure.)

MOST books on British local government include towards the end a short chapter on the place of party politics in local government. This reflects their relative importance in the local government scene, because although they are of great significance in the affairs of the larger councils they do not occupy that central position which is accorded to them in West Africa; especially is this true of the smaller urban and district councils with which the West African ones can best be compared. So overwhelming is the importance of party politics in West African local government, however, that a chapter on the subject deserves a more prominent place, even though it need not be very long; for here we have another radical departure from what used to be called the British model.

It is a fact often noticed by West African observers that elections in the county boroughs, counties and many municipal councils in Britain are fought on a basis of party politics. What sometimes escapes the observers is the true significance of this fact. Party politics entered local government in Britain when local authorities began to handle affairs of national importance on which Conservatives, Socialists and Liberals normally differ. They do not normally differ, on grounds of political ideology, on such matters as disposing of refuse, keeping the streets clean, repairing the roads, or providing markets, maternity and child welfare centres, pure water supplies, public transport or other amenities; though with the growth of a complex urban civilization differences can begin to appear even in some of these. But broadly speaking what was required was honest and efficient administration, and over a very wide area of local authority work right-wing Conservatives and left-wing Socialists would be hard put to it to discover reasons, based on political belief, for disagreeing with each other. Consequently, in the earlier days of local government little was heard of party politics and the majority of councillors were simply people who wanted their neighbourhood to be well provided for.

But the growth of party politics in British local government was inevitable, and proper, because local authorities carry the main burden of administration in most of the major social services, and their responsibilities now go far beyond providing non-controversial amenities; they must prepare long-term schemes for education, slum clearance, town planning and housing, the use and development of land, and the provision of services like water, electricity and hospitals which have a national rather than a local implication; the last two have in fact been 'nationalized', that is responsibility for them has been transferred from local to central government because they could only be effectively provided for over a wider area than that covered by a local council. In matters of this magnitude it is sensible that local politics should reflect national politics. There are, for example, very real differences in political belief about what sort of education system there should be, whether land and property should be compulsorily acquired in the public interest, or what proportion of houses should be built by public and private enterprise; and these are all matters in which the larger local councils have a considerable measure of independent responsibility.

The point is that whether party politics in local government is right or wrong depends on what the councils do. In West Africa this has not been a relevant consideration;

in the first place, few councils perform duties which have more than a local significance; in the second, political parties do not in fact differ on how things should be done, but simply on who should do them.

A study of the minute book of almost any council will show that the greater part of the business of the council and its committees is concerned with such matters as the appointment and personal affairs of the staff, councillors' allowances, the award of contracts, the repair of roads, the allocation of market stalls and comparable matters. None of them could be called political in the sense that there are different *ideological* points of view as to how they should be done and who should do them. It is difficult to suppose, for example, that there is a party political method of sweeping the market, cutting the grass and filling in holes in the road; yet some small councils which have done little more than this have done it in an atmosphere of bitter political warfare. This leads to the second point, that political parties are not divided from each other by social and economic policies and beliefs, but by personalities and ethnic rivalries. The fight to win local council elections does not turn on establishing rival plans for social progress, but on entrenching a party in power in a particular locality and winning appointments and perquisites for party supporters. Local councils tend to resemble what in Britain would be called the 'constituency organizations' of a party. The point is worth dwelling on for a moment. In any British town there will be a town council, which may have either a Conservative or a Socialist majority; but if it is a large town, and the centre of a parliamentary constituency, the Conservative and Labour parties may well have local offices and professional party organizers, whose function is to keep the local party organization in good repair, raise funds, recruit members, disseminate propaganda and prepare to win the next general election. There is, however, no connection between, say the Conservative town council and the local headquarters of the Conservative party. In the first the Conservative councillors hammer out, under the criticism of their Socialist opponents, how to provide the *town* with social services; in the other they plan to defeat the Socialists at the next general election in the *parliamentary constituency*. This might or might not correspond with the area of the local authority; in a large town there might be two or more parliamentary constituencies, whereas a small town might be incorporated in a much larger rural area.

In West Africa, on the other hand, the council has often tended to *become* the constituency party organization.

The difference may be illustrated by another important convention, which is widely, though not universally, observed in Britain. In a 'borough', that is a town which has a mayor, it is customary either for the mayor to come from the majority party and the deputy mayor from the minority one, or for the two parties to hold the office in turn; this symbolizes the fact that the mayor is the chief representative citizen and is to that extent above politics. Similarly, it is customary either to share the chairmanships of committees between the parties, or to arrange that the chairman comes from one party and the vice-chairman from another; it is also customary to spread the membership of the committees proportionately between the parties. Incidentally, it is the general experience that in committees dealing with the down-to-earth work of local government party differences tend to evaporate, while in small councils dealing with purely local matters they hardly exist at all; in such councils there is still room for the politically independent member.

The contrast in West African councils is sharp. Not only does the winning party take all the chairmanships, but unless restrained they will appoint only party members to committees; we have already seen (p. 89) that the Western Nigerian Government was once compelled to include a section in its local government law enabling the Minister to use powers of direction if it appeared to him 'that the minority parties are not adequately represented on a committee of the council'; otherwise they might well have been excluded altogether. The power of the majority party used to pervade every aspect of a council's life and work, even to the extent of compelling the council's employees to join the party under threat of dismissal.

In general, throughout this book, we are not concerned to criticize departures from British practice; indeed, we have several times stressed the point that foreign institutions cannot be imported with any hope of success unless they are applied flexibly and are readily adapted to suit local circumstances and tradition, and most of the adaptations that have been made so far are more suitable than the original. We are tempted to make an exception here, because the influence of party politics on local government is so manifestly bad. Councils are diverted from their proper purposes; members or supporters of other parties are victimized; and no moderation is shown.

We do not suggest that the problem is easy or straightforward, because if local government develops to the extent of administering services of national importance, and of a controversial kind, party politics will come to have a legitimate place. Even now, people in West Africa ask how local authorities can act as agents of the central government if they have a different political loyalty. This question makes two assumptions; first, that political beliefs are involved in the matters on which governments and local authorities deal with one another, which is, as we have seen, largely untrue; second, that the local authorities are in fact agents of the central government, which is only partly true. Nevertheless, it is a fact that in Britain as elsewhere a special difficulty may arise when a council of one political complexion has to carry out the policies of a government of another; it need not necessarily arise, because a great deal of the work involved between them is non-controversial; but it can very well arise, and frequently does so. A high proportion of town councils in Britain today have Socialist majorities, whereas the Government is a Conservative one, and occasionally they have had sharp differences.

When this happens the only solution is moderation and restraint. The Government must, of course, have the final word, since there can only be one sovereign authority in the state, since local councils draw their own authority from Parliament, and since they depend to a large extent on the Government for money. But a government, of whatever party, will be careful not to prevent councils from following their own convictions, and not to compel them to act against these convictions, except in matters which they consider to be really vital; local councils for their part will acknowledge the authority of the government of the day, and will not seek to press differences to the point of deadlock or collapse. In West Africa it has been all too common in the past for those who have to accept something they do not like to 'walk out' and refuse to take any further part in the proceedings; this does nothing to further either the welfare of their constituents or the cause of democracy.

It is often thought that compromise of this kind is a typically British escape from a difficult situation, that the British have elevated it to a virtue among their own people, and that they have no business to force it down the throats of Africans. It is significant, therefore, that one of the best statements of the principle involved was once made by the Premier of the Northern Region of Nigeria, in 1958. In a message headed 'Declaration by the government of the Northern Region on its relations with native authorities', the late Sardauna of Sokoto said:

'During the recent tours of the Premier, at some places he was asked to clarify the position of native authorities and the Regional government in a self-governing Northern Region, and therefore the Premier takes this chance to make the stand of the government known not only to those who asked but to everybody in the Region.

'In every country where there are democratic institutions the relationship between the Government in power and local government bodies is bound to present certain problems. Nigeria is no exception to this rule. The

Regional government therefore believes that a clear statement of its policy on this subject will be of value in allaying any doubts which may exist among native authorities and political parties of the Opposition.

'The government of the Northern Region recognizes that, just as the constitution provides different spheres of activity for the Federal government on the one hand and the Regional government on the other, so the law defines separate fields for the Regional government on the one hand and the native authorities on the other. Within the field of local government, the Regional government is ready to grant native authorities complete freedom of action provided always that certain essential conditions are observed. These conditions are that native authorities should retain the confidence of the great mass of their people, that they should discharge adequately the duties and responsibilities assigned to them, that they should conduct their financial affairs in a prudent and responsible fashion, and that they should maintain the standards of honesty and impartiality required in a country approaching independence.

'The Regional government, which is ultimately responsible for law, order and sound administration must, however, reserve to itself the right to intervene in local government matters if these conditions are not met. This right is recognized by the law which has provided certain overriding powers. These are financial, executive and legal, and they vary in range from the ability to withhold a small grant to the power of the Governor-in-Council to annul the appointment of any native authority.

'Wide as these powers are, however, they cannot be arbitrarily exercised. They are subject to two great sanctions of democratic representative government, namely the rule of law and freedom of discussion. Native authorities are constituted under and safeguarded by legal processes and any government which sought to suppress them or encroach upon their statutory rights would have to proceed according to law. Such a move, whether justified or not, would be reported in the Press and could be made the subject of a debate in the regional legislature. Consequently any government which took action against a native authority from improper motives would risk exposure at the bar of public opinion.

'These are the safeguards which democracy provides to preserve the weak against the strong and they are just as important in constitutional as in human relationships. The Regional government affirms its faith in these safeguards and pledges itself to observe them in the spirit as well as the letter. In particular it is resolved to treat all native authorities, irrespective of their political sympathies, with strict impartiality and scrupulously to refrain from any action which could be attributed to political bias. Native authorities may therefore rest assured that, provided that they for their part discharge their statutory and moral obligations, they will not be subject to unjustifiable interference or undue influence by the Regional government.'

This sums up the situation admirably.

Finally, it must not be thought that party politics have entered British local government, at any level, without protest or regret. Two main arguments have been advanced against them; first, that the need to be sponsored as a candidate by a political party has robbed local government of the services of many men and women who would have been an asset to it, but who belong to no political party, or at any rate are not politically active; and second, that party organization within the council, with its 'caucus' and its voting on strict party lines, robs the council debates of any reality and means that all the decisions are taken in advance. The first of these arguments is a substantial one in a country where many citizens of great ability and public spirit have not the obsessive interest in politics that one finds in West Africa; the second applies equally to the House of Commons; the argument and discussion out of which policy is shaped take place within the party and not within the whole elected body, and there is both loss and gain in this.

But the argument that the *major* local authorities are now dealing with matters which may properly be called political is conclusive; added to which party politics have added a good deal of interest and zest to the work of local councils, and, judging from the proportion of electors who take the trouble to vote in local elections (never very high), have also increased the interest of the electorate.

But to repeat, and in conclusion, two conditions need to be observed; first, that party politics are confined to matters which are in essence political, and should not be allowed to dominate every aspect of a local authority's work, much less affect the staff and the routine work; and second, that political power should be used with moderation, and that councillors of the opposition should not be excluded from a fair share of responsibility.

CHAPTER 7

The Revenue of Local Authorities

WE have glanced at some of the ways in which local authorities may *spend* their money, though it has been impossible to make any useful generalizations because work is shared differently in different countries between central and local government.

When we turn to the question of how they *get* their money it is equally difficult to generalize. We can, however, say in very broad terms that their sources of revenue are threefold—government grants, locally imposed taxes and miscellaneous receipts; the first two account for about 80%, though in proportions which differ from one place to another. Let us look briefly at each of these three in turn.

Government Grants

The relationship between central and local government can to some extent be deduced from the amount of grant aid which a government gives to local authorities. In Britain the Government has for many years been contributing more than half, though there is some variation as between one kind of public service and another. This is partly because in a small country standards in the more important public services have got to be national rather than local, and by being, so to speak, the biggest local ratepayer the Government is in a position to see that standards are maintained; but it means that local government as a whole has lost a great deal of its historic independence. In many other countries, among them Canada and the United States, New Zealand, Sweden, West Germany and Switzerland, the average amount raised locally is about 70%, and local government is proportionately more independent. In West Africa government grant was at one time exceeding 50% in the former Eastern Region of Nigeria, but in the West and in Ghana it never rose above 40%, and as government spending became more ambitious it tended to decline. It was lowest of all in the old Northern Region, but this was because of the dominant importance that the former Native Authorities had always had in the administration of the country; it was the only part of West Africa where local government had played a rôle comparable to that in the United Kingdom. Ten years ago, out of a total NA revenue of nearly £12 million less than £1½ million came from Government.

Grant aid can be given in several ways, but there are two principal ones. First it may be a *percentage* of what the service is going to cost. The percentage type of grant may be illustrated from former practice in Western Nigeria.

This is an area, it will be recalled, where there were local government police forces, and in order to assist councils to maintain them, and also to give the Government a right to inspect them, the Government paid for 50% of their recurrent costs; they also paid 25% of their capital costs, that is the cost of such things as new buildings and equipment, as distinct from pay and annual upkeep. The health services for which the local authorities were responsible, on the other hand, received only 10%, recurrent and capital. It could be argued, though this is speculative, that these facts indicated that the Government regarded the maintenance of law and order as having a greater national significance than the local sanitary services and dispensaries. This principle could certainly be seen in the grants for the upkeep of roads, for these varied from nil for local laterite roads to £84 per mile for the most important 'provincial' roads, with many graduations in between; the wider the use to which the road was put the greater the percentage grant. The same principle could be seen, though applied in a slightly different way, in the service which was regarded as being the most important of all, namely education; for here the Government paid 100% of the salaries of primary school teachers, local education officers, supervising teachers and their essential staff, leaving the local authorities themselves to bear the cost of maintaining the schools in good repair. It was interesting, incidentally, that in this Region, which has a 'unified local government service' for certain grades, the Government paid 50% of their salaries. To take a quite different kind of example, this is a Region which in its coastal areas relies a good deal on waterways for transport, and the Government paid 50% of the cost of keeping them navigable.

This system of percentage grants is universal, and the example of Western Nigeria has been used merely to give it a little local colour. It is not, however, without its problems, and the trend in Britain at the moment is away from percentage grants, and towards a different kind of grant which we will discuss in a moment. Its worst defect is that it tends to help the rich authorities proportionately more than the poorer ones. In private life, if someone offers you £1 for £1 to help you to buy a car, his offer will not help you to buy a very good car if you can only scrape together £100 yourself. Similarly, an offer of 50% grant aid for a certain service will help richer authorities to provide a very good service but will still impose a limit on what can be done in a poorer area, where the service may be much more greatly needed.

To overcome this defect, governments in Britain and other countries have devised what are called 'equalization' grants, designed to give a higher proportion of aid to those authorities which are naturally poor than to those which are naturally rich. This type of grant in Britain was started thirty years ago in circumstances which are not relevant to this discussion; indeed, they have now greatly altered, and the method of calculating the grant has several times been changed. But the principle remains. There are certain areas which because of their past history or their local natural resources are worse off financially than others, and it is just in these places, which can least afford them, that expensive social services are most needed. To meet this difficulty a formula was devised which took into account the main factors which held back development and which caused expensive services to be needed. These factors were the rate of local unemployment, the proportion of children to adults in the population (since children are the cause of some of the most expensive services), the way in which the value of property in the council's area compared with the average for the whole country, and the degree to which the area of the authority was scattered or compact, since distances are one of the factors which add to expense; this last calculation, incidentally, was made on the basis of 'population per road mile'.

It is obvious that a calculation of this kind is a very complicated one, which could not be made without a tremendous volume of reliable statistical information. This is important from the West African point of view, because the same problem of natural inequality is at least as great there as in Britain. Some authorities are, for example, in wealthy cocoa-growing areas, where the general level of prosperity is high; others may be in semi-desert areas where people exist on their cattle and a little subsistence agriculture, or, by contrast, in crowded towns with heavy unemployment and a serious lack of urban social services. From the point of view of national equality some should receive more grant aid from the Government than others, and a straightforward percentage grant, while naturally helping everybody, might make the actual disparity between rich and poor greater instead of less. Unfortunately the statistical information which is needed to devise a fair equalization grant is still very largely lacking in West Africa, and equalization grants, though accepted in principle, have to be based on very crude calculations, usually the simple one of the estimated relative population of the different authorities.

The Federal Government of Nigeria faced a similar problem in devising how the Federal revenue derived from import and export duties should be distributed to the Regions on the principle of 'need', as distinct from that of 'derivation'. The principle of need means that a certain proportion of this revenue is paid to the Regions not because the produce was exported from them, or because the imported goods are being purchased by them, but because one Region is in greater need than another from natural causes. Here is a very comparable situation, on the national level, where an equalization formula is necessary; but the calculation can only be based on two factors, both rather 'rough and ready', the estimated population and the estimated income per head.

Reverting to percentage grants, their other weakness is that they detract from the independence of local authorities to spend their money in the way they think fit. If most of the grant revenue is in the form of percentage aid for specific services their policy of development is very largely dictated for them, except in relatively minor matters in which they find all the money themselves; in which case they are indeed in danger of becoming 'mere agents' of the Government. It is this argument which has recently caused the Government of Britain to abolish most percentage grants in favour of grants which amount to very much the same in total, but which can be spent more at the discretion of the local councils, a decision which has provoked a great deal of controversy. However, there has always been controversy about the relative merits of percentage grants and the other kind of grant (usually called the 'block' grant) which has 'no strings attached', and policy has leaned now in one direction and now in another. The percentage grant is likely to be of particular value in an undeveloped country, because it is useful for getting new services started—services which may be unpopular or little understood, and which would have little chance of being developed if they had to depend entirely on local initiative; the block grant is more suitable for assisting a responsible and well-developed authority to keep its services going.

However, block grants are already established in West Africa alongside percentage grants.

There are no fixed rules about the ways in which grant aid may be given, but simply certain well-established practices. Percentage grants and block grants have been discussed in a little detail because they are the most usual, but governments may make any variations that may seem to them expedient in different circumstances. Many grants are of a special or *ad hoc* kind, given once and for all for a particular purpose, especially for capital expenditure. For example, Western Nigeria used to give local authorities 40% of the cost of rural health centres, 50% of urban water supplies and 100% for rural water supplies, but the arrangements for maintaining these services varied considerably; in the case of urban water supplies the Government gave a subsidy which would keep the local water rate below a certain figure which it was believed the inhabitants can afford.

There is accordingly room for infinite variety in the matter of Government grants, and the important thing is not so much to learn precisely how they are awarded at any particular time and place, because this is constantly changing, but to appreciate the principles which govern their award.

Local tax (or 'rate')

Although local authorities may receive some 40–50% of their revenue from Government grants, and although there are good reasons why this should be so, it is obvious that if local government is going to have any real meaning the authorities must be able to raise a comparable amount from their own resources, which of course they do. The most important item of this 'home-produced' revenue is the local tax on individual income or property, which is usually known as a 'rate'; in certain cases, such as an education or water rate, it is a payment for a specific service.

Unfortunately the local rate, when it is levied upon an

individual's income as distinct from his property, is still apt to become entangled with the central income tax assessed and collected by the Inland Revenue Department or its equivalent, and it is not always easy to disentangle the two. It is certainly impossible to make a brief general statement which will cover all three countries, as their history and present practice in this respect vary so much. It was the general practice in colonial days for the native authorities to collect the tax (there being only one kind of tax) and for the proceeds to be divided between the Government and the native authority, each taking a fixed percentage. Often this arrangement worked well for the native authorities, who were allowed to keep a high proportion, and sometimes the whole, but the proportion was inclined to vary according to the financial pressures on the governments at any given time, and the whole tax belonged in principle to the governments; as people became wealthier, and the assessment of a *graduated* tax became more complicated, it was clear that the native authorities, and the local authorities which succeeded them, were not really as competent to work a system of graduated income tax as they had been to collect the 'flat' tax of earlier days; too much was required in the way of staff, information and office organization. Accordingly income tax departments grew up in the central governments for the purpose of collecting a tax from people of easily ascertainable incomes, or from traders and merchants who moved from place to place, or from expatriates, or from commercial firms, or from others for whom the simple apparatus of the local authority's tax office was inappropriate. Broadly speaking income tax would go to the Government and local rates to the local authority, but unfortunately the actual position is not as simple as this. In Western Nigeria the local authorities used to collect income tax from the great majority of individual taxpayers (though not the special, and wealthier, categories) but were allowed by the Government to retain the whole of it. In Eastern Nigeria the central government became the taxing authority in 1956, and for some years afterwards the local rate, imposed in addition, had to be kept down by the Government in order not to prejudice the collection of income tax. In Ghana the position was that the machinery of central government income tax gradually worked downwards, as it became easier to ascertain more and more individual incomes, and as the techniques of assessment and collection improved.[1]

But however it was done, the Instruments of all the major local authorities declared them to be 'rating authorities', and gave them not only the power to levy rates but the positive duty to collect sufficient rates for the services which they budgeted to provide. There were several ways in which they might do this, which were set out in great detail in the local government laws of Southern Nigeria and Ghana; it is not easy to summarize these laws, since they differed in their arrangement and there were indeed some differences in substance between them. With variations, however, they allowed councils to impose rates in the following ways:

A capitation rate

This is the oldest form of rating in these countries, dating from early colonial days, and it used to be called by such names as 'head' or 'poll' tax. It is now generally regarded as an archaic form of taxation, but provision is still made for it, since there are still many people who ought to be taxed but whose income is small and not easily ascertainable. In Nigeria it was imposed on people over sixteen years of age and in Ghana over eighteen. In Western Nigeria the assumption was made that everybody who appeared to be taxable must have a minimum income of £50 p.a., and the capitation rate was fixed at £1 17s 6d; in Eastern Nigeria it was reduced to 5s when the Government took over responsibility for central taxation, but it later rose to about £1. But although it remains, and will

---

[1] For an excellent study of this whole subject, which it is impossible to summarize here, see G. Oka Orewa: *Taxation in Western Nigeria*, NISER—OUP, 1962.

be a valuable source of revenue for some time to come, it is more and more giving way to the second form of local rating, i.e.

A rate on assessable income

This gets away from the unsatisfactory principle of everyone paying the same and introduces the principle of paying what they can afford on a graduated scale, and it is quite simply a form of local income tax. It was assessed by local assessment committees of the councils, an arrangement which had some unsatisfactory features, being among other things extremely open to corruption, though in Western Nigeria, for example, this was improved because of the advice and supervision given by the Regional Tax Board. The principle of a graduated tax is sound, though as countries develop local rates on income are probably more appropriate to rural than to urban areas, which are likely to rely more and more on rates on fixed property.

These rates on individuals are intended for the general revenue of the councils, to enable them to meet a wide range of commitments.

A Special Rate

This expression can have two meanings:

(*a*) It can mean a rate levied upon everybody in a council area for a special purpose, such as a school or a water supply (to name the two most usual). In Britain rates of this kind have largely died away, because it is simpler and cheaper to collect one consolidated rate, and people who like to know how their money is being spent can always learn, because the facts are printed on the rate demand note in very great detail. But this cannot yet be done in West Africa, and although no one in any country enjoys paying his rates it has been found from experience that the special rate is popular, or at any rate people object to paying it less than they do the general rate. This is a point of some importance among unsophisticated people; they resent having to pay a rate for the general purposes of the council, because they cannot understand what happens to the money and are suspicious—sometimes rightly —that it will be wasted; but if they are told that in return for paying a special rate they will get a school or a standpipe they will pay willingly. Like all of us they like to see something for their money.

(*b*) It can also mean a rate levied upon people living in certain parts of a local authority area, and not over the whole area. This is especially appropriate in rural areas, where a service may be provided in part of the area but not the whole. If a certain village is provided by the council with a supply of piped water, people in another village ten miles away who are still carrying buckets to a stream will not be enthusiastic about paying for it, even if they do happen to be in the same council area.

A Rate on Property

This is an increasingly important kind of rate, especially in urban areas. Property means in effect buildings, whether they are dwelling houses, offices, shops, cinemas or indeed almost any kind of premises, though the Ghana Act did in fact permit a rate to be assessed on 'possessions, or any category of possessions'.

Rates on property are the basis of local taxation in more developed countries, and especially in Britain where there are no rates on local income. Although like any form of taxation they occasionally give rise to anomalies and injustices, they are thought to be the best basis for local rating, chiefly because the revenue derived from them is permanent, dependable and foreseeable. They are based on the idea that the owner (or in the case of dwelling houses it may be the owner or occupier) should pay a rate which is related to the value of his property. There are several alternative ways of assessing what this value is, and different countries use different systems. In Britain valuation is based on a calculation of what rent the property would command if it were let. In Ghana it was the estimated capital value of the property; for example, if a house is thought to be worth £500, allowance having been made for depreciation, a rateable value would be calculated from this and a rate of the order of 6d or 1s in the £ charged upon it; if the calculation were based on 10% of the capital value the rate would accordingly be 25s or 50s. To take an example from Eastern Nigeria, a larger and better type of house might be valued at £2,000 and under the formula once in use in that Region its rateable value might be assessed at £100 p.a.; a customary rate could well be 2s in the £, which would make the owner liable to an annual rate of £10. In Sierra Leone there was a simpler calculation; houses made of mud and wattle with a thatch or bamboo roof were valued at £1 per room per annum; a corrugated iron roof and mud blocks would send it up to £3 per room; concrete or timber walls to £5 or £10, according to the construction of the roof; if the rate levied by town councils was 3s in the £, a two-roomed house in the lowest category would pay 3s in the £ on £2, i.e. 6s; whereas a four-roomed house in the highest category would pay 3s on £40, i.e. £6. Business premises were usually rated as so much per square foot, according to the purpose of the building and its locality in the town, a principle which can also be applied to dwelling houses.

The possible variations are enormous, and the whole question of property rating is a highly specialized study. Even the process of valuing property for rating purposes requires expert knowledge, as is shown by the fact that in Ghana experts have been recruited from the United Nations Technical Assistance Organization to train Ghanaian valuers; the valuation of Freetown for property rating occupied a large team of valuers over five years.

Property rating has not made very much headway yet in West Africa, but it is spreading at an accelerating pace. In Ghana 'it is becoming increasingly popular and its further development is only limited by the number of valuers available to assess the property'.[2] In Eastern

[2] A. F. Greenwood, *Journal of Local Administration Overseas*, January 1962: 'Ten Years of Local Government in Ghana.'

Nigeria it used to operate in the eight largest towns, the valuation being made by the local councils, with guiding rules supplied by the Government valuer. It has made most progress in the present Mid-West State, where it is established in Benin, Warri, Sapele, Ughelli and Agbor; in the Western State it was accepted ten years ago in principle for the vital city of Ibadan, but the principle had not yet been put into practice. In Sierra Leone it applies in a few of the main 'townships' in addition to Freetown, the valuation being done by leading members of the town councils.

We must leave the subject of rating here, although it requires a book to itself. There is space only for two general comments. First, the various kinds of rates which we have just outlined may give the impression that local government may well cost the individual a small fortune, especially when it is remembered that personal *and* property rates may be levied at the same time; the question arises of what it is reasonable that a man should pay to his local council for local services. Very little research has been done into what he actually does pay in relation to his total income. In Britain, at a very rough calculation, the ordinary man living in a council house might pay about two weeks' wages in the year in local rates, but he gets a good deal more in return for his money than most Africans; some calculations in Western Nigeria proceeded on the basis that 5% of income 'to the public purse' would be reasonable, whereas in Ghana the yardstick used by local authorities was 1% of assessable income for *local* tax, subject to an upward limit of £5. Everything turns, of course, on 'value for money'; people will pay cheerfully if they see results and will try to evade their obligations if they don't. This leads to the second point, that throughout West Africa in town and 'bush' alike, arrears of rates are an unceasing and apparently insoluble problem. 'Tax drives' are constantly being used to get in as much as possible in order to avoid financial crises, but nowhere are the general rates paid regularly, promptly and without trouble. This, we must hope, is a matter of education, and that it will improve as understanding of public affairs develops, but few people at the moment seem able to realize the effects of rate arrears, in the non-payment of salaries and the suspension of public services.

Methods of assessment

A little more needs to be said about the assessment, or the calculation of the amount, of the rate. In the case of capitation or income rates this means calculating how much each individual shall pay, and this, as we have said, is usually done by local assessment committees; in the case of property rating it means deciding how many shillings and pence in the £ shall be charged on the annual value of the property, however this may be determined. The actual *valuation* is sometimes done by the Inland Revenue Department of the Government (which is now the British practice) and sometimes by a committee of the councils themselves (which used to be the British practice, but which was abandoned in order to get greater national uniformity). But the *assessment* is done by the local authorities themselves, in their capacity of rating authorities, and it is one of their most important responsibilities. It must be remembered, however, that councils' estimates are subject to the approval of the Government, and in practice governments have often had to restrain councils from making a rate which they (the governments) thought unreasonably high, and have tried to establish a more or less uniform level of assessment throughout the country. This is especially true of personal, as distinct from property, rating in the rural areas, where councils in the first flush of enthusiasm, and in their desire to create improvements in their area, often overestimated the ratepayers' willingness, or even ability, to pay.

In spite of the restraining arm of government, however, the annual fixing of the rate is an important event in the work of any council, and it is necessary to understand how they set about it, for there is a change here from the old days of native administration. The NA used to sit down once a year and decide what the tax ought to be, i.e. how much people could afford to pay; having added up what this would come to they then worked out how much they could afford to spend, and what to spend it on. Local authorities today adopt the more progressive approach of first working out what they want and how much it would cost; they then consider the total value of the property which is subject to rating, or the incomes of the people subject to income rating, and the number of people subject to capitation rating, and then work out what the rate would have to be fixed at if they were to be able to do what they wanted. Of course they are limited by what is possible and they generally finish by having to 'cut their coat according to their cloth', but there is none the less a very important difference in the two approaches to the problem. It should be added that there is usually provision for ratepayers to appeal against their assessment, for certain people, e.g. the old or infirm, to be exempted from rating, and for certain kinds of property, e.g. churches or community centres, to receive preferential assessment.

MINOR SOURCES OF REVENUE

Grants and rates account between them for more than 80% of the revenue of local authorities, but there remains 20% or so which comes from other sources, and this is not an inconsiderable amount. It is raised in miscellaneous ways.

A large proportion of it may come from the administration of the local courts, in fines and fees, though the expenses of the court have to be set against this and it is quite possible for there to be a deficit instead of a surplus. It is not a good principle that the revenue of the courts should come to be relied on as income for local government, and it is something of an anomaly that while the personnel of the courts has been separated from that of the councils their finances are still so closely intertwined. Obviously the local authorities must be reimbursed for the cost of

maintaining the courts, which is one of their statutory
duties, but the principle of financing local services from
the profits of crime is open to question and could lead to
abuses.

Another source of revenue is from fees charged for
specific services, which ought to be paid for by the
individuals who use them rather than by the whole community in the form of rates. Examples are the fees for
car or lorry parks, for the use of slaughter houses or for
market stalls (although these could more properly be called
rents). These, however, should not be regarded as a significant source of revenue, as the real purpose of charging
fees is to defray the cost of providing the service, e.g.
paying the wages of supervisors, attendants or cleaners; in
principle the object should be to provide the service at the
lowest cost rather than to think of it as a source of general
revenue. The same principle should apply to the larger
undertakings of the big cities, e.g. the fares charged for a
municipal bus service should be as low as is consistent with
maintaining and improving the service and setting aside
enough money for depreciation and replacements; some
bus services can be highly profitable, and there is a temptation for the authority to regard them as a source of revenue
for general purposes instead of a service to the people who
use them.

Then there are various kinds of 'licences', which may be
for such varied purposes as bicycles, carts, canoes, palm-wine shops, bakeries, slaughter houses, firearms, drumming
or entertainments. Here again there is apt to be a confusion
of principle. The purpose of making people take out
licences ought to be either because it is undesirable to have
too many of a certain thing, e.g. palm-wine sellers or
hawkers; or because there is something potentially
dangerous or insanitary which ought to be inspected and
controlled, like firearms on the one hand or bakeries and
slaughter houses on the other. While it is convenient to
treat these as sources of income there needs to be a sense
of moderation. There is a temptation to want to licence,

for the sake of the fees, certain things which are really helping to develop the country, and which ought to be encouraged rather than taxed. In countries with very little public transport, bicycles are an advantage, as are any forms of vehicle which can replace the inefficient system of head-loading. The licensing principle, when applied to these, is more open to question, for it may amount to a tax on progress.

Lastly, some local authorities, though by no means all, derive revenue from such things as the sale of timber or firewood from forest reserves, local industries such as weaving and pottery, and the profits of seed nurseries or agricultural plots; while the larger urban authorities often earn a considerable revenue from rents and leases.

Nevertheless it is the general and special rate, backed by central government grants, which is the foundation of local authority revenue.

LOANS

So far we have spoken almost entirely in terms of the recurrent revenue which councils need for their work, though we mentioned in passing that Government grants may include grants for capital expenditure. But major capital developments cannot be financed in this way, and councils which aspire to more ambitious schemes, such as a large-scale market development, a drainage scheme or a town hall would normally try to raise a loan, the interest and capital of which would be repaid over a long period of years. Here again there has been a significant change from the old days of native administration, for NAs were not allowed to borrow, and if they wanted to spend money they first had to save it little by little out of annual surpluses (which were obligatory); this obviously held back development. It has since been realized that borrowing, subject of course to adequate security for the loan, offers the only way to make progress. It is also more equitable than paying for large capital projects out of savings, for the people who will enjoy the benefits of the project are the coming generations, who can reasonably be expected to pay for it out of the rates that they will pay in future years.

The sections of the local government laws which deal with borrowing were almost identical. Councils may raise loans, subject to the prior approval of the Minister, from any proper source within the country—the Government itself, the banks or public corporations established for the purpose; the security for the loan is 'the property and revenues of the council', and there were naturally stringent provisions in the law about councils which defaulted on the payment of interest or capital. The extent to which loans can be raised is of course limited by the amount of loan capital which is available in the country and by the creditworthiness of the councils. Nevertheless a good many useful projects of the kind mentioned have been financed by loans of the order of £100,000, which means that progress has been made which could never have been made in the days when native authorities had to save before they could spend. If the projects themselves are revenue-producing, like a big market or a bus service, or in the longer term like a drainage scheme or a road, their repayment is not necessarily a great burden on future generations, and the Minister would have a strong preference for sanctioning loans of this kind, rather than for projects which have a greater social than economic value, or whose economic benefit cannot be calculated except in terms of the distant future. Nevertheless, social projects are not necessarily excluded, and in Eastern Nigeria loans used to be raised for health centres, river craft, water supplies and 'Bailey bridges' as well as for projects whose economic advantages were more immediate.

A short chapter of a short book cannot deal properly with such a vast subject as local government finance, but the foregoing is a bare sketch of the more important aspects of the subject, so far as revenue is concerned.

PART II

Most of the references to Ghana in this Part of the book have been nullified by the military *coup* of January, 1972, and are now of historical significance only.

CHAPTER 8

The Cities of West Africa

THE differences between local government in the bigger cities and local government in the bush are so profound that it is more appropriate to discuss Freetown, Accra, Lagos, Ibadan and Kaduna in the same chapter than in the chapters on the countries of which they happen to be the capitals. Throughout the world local government in any highly organized sense has begun in towns and cities[1] and only later has it spread to the countryside or bush; throughout the world problems of city administration are similar, whereas those of rural local government are infinitely varied. Urban local government is much the more vital, in the literal sense that without municipal sanitation people would die of disease; without municipal housing they would die of exposure; without municipal street and traffic control modern life would grind slowly to a halt; and without municipal amenities life would hardly be worth living at all. Municipal sanitation and the rest are an *advantage* in the bush, but life could go on without them, as it has done for centuries; in the big cities life would stop. Indeed, as we suggested in the first chapter, the function of local government in the bush is to stimulate economic development rather than to provide essential services.

Furthermore, in the particular circumstances of West

[1] In the English language as applied to British local government there is no important difference between the words 'city' and 'town'. Generally speaking 'city' implies a larger place, and certainly a place of greater status and prestige. But there is no administrative difference and the words are often used indiscriminately. The word 'municipal', used later in the chapter, literally applies to local government of any kind, but is customarily applied to urban as distinct from rural administration.

Africa conciliar local government ought to have striking advantages in town as compared with country. A far higher proportion of the people are educated and versed in business or bureaucratic ways, and there is a professional, merchant and middle class from which competent councillors could be recruited; and while the revenues available are pathetically small in relation to the huge tasks waiting to be performed they are more than enough to provide responsible work for councillors and officials alike. They cannot be said to have responded to the challenge, for throughout West Africa the record of incompetence and corruption has been worse in the cities than anywhere else, and a few years ago there was scarcely a town of any size which was not being examined by some commission or other for maladministration and corruption. It is perhaps unfortunate that Governments in recent years have poured so much energy into establishing modern local government in the rural areas—spreading it thinly, so to speak, over the entire map—that they failed in what might have been the more profitable task of developing sound municipal administration in the cities. Certainly the typical twentieth-century problems—uncontrolled growth, pollution, slums, congestion, and the breakdown of public services through over-strain—are as acute in West Africa as anywhere in the world.

Lagos

Lagos itself might well be used as a model to illustrate all the most intractable problems that trouble urban administrators in the 1970s. Although not large by the standards of the great cities of the world it is probably one of the fastest growing. The last census in 1963 gave a population of 665,000 within the formal city boundaries, but these have little relation to the real built-up area and it was calculated that another 425,000 ought to have been added to give the population of the continuous conurbation; the figure today could well be a million and a half, for recent research has shown that population within the city limits is growing at about 8% per annum, while in the urbanizing areas beyond it is nearly 20%, which must be one of the highest figures in the world. Indeed the authors of the research into growth[2] have said: 'The history of Africa records no previous movement of comparable magnitude.'

Growth has been unplanned and largely unforeseen and has gathered such momentum that it is impossible to halt or reverse it, and there seems no reason why by the end of the century the built-up area should not stretch ten miles inland, or as far as Ikorodu. The penalty that the public has to pay is constant failure of water and electricity, chaotic traffic, inadequate public transport, and tiring and expensive journeys to work. The vital part of the city is on a crowded island, connected with the mainland by two bridges, a few feet only above sea-level. In the whole enormous complex there is no modern sewage disposal plant, and the cost of installing one would be astronomical. The administrators of Lagos therefore face a gigantic task by any standards in the world. What form, then, does local administration take?

As so often happens—and as had happened notably in the United Kingdom in the last twenty-five years—it derives from structures designed to meet the needs of simpler days, and now largely obsolete. The Lagos Town (now City) Council is a body of long standing, but until the 1960s it was in essence a sanitary, public health and markets authority only; it then acquired other responsibilities, notably a bus service purchased from private enterprise and the administration of primary education. More recently still its social welfare and works programmes have greatly increased, and its budget is now in the neighbourhood of £5½ million, four or five times what it was ten years ago. Nevertheless it could not possibly undertake responsibility for providing the major public services or solving the major planning problems of the city. For many years the Ministry of Lagos Affairs of the Federal Government was responsible

[2] The Physical Planning Research Unit of the Nigerian Institute of Social and Economic Research, University of Ibadan.

for the major roads and streets and for the vital water supply, and has now been succeeded by the Lagos State Government; the Ports Authority is responsible for the City's most important undertaking; the Electricity Corporation supplies it with electricity; and the statutory corporation known as the Lagos Executive Devolopment Board, originally capitalized by the Federal Government and the Colonial Development Corporation, has been responsible for the huge undertaking of clearing the worst of the slums, replanning the City centre and creating new housing estates on the outskirts.

Here is an example of five different 'agencies', all within the same geographical area, performing functions best suited to the different kinds of work and to the resources which each can command. Unfortunately the division of labour between them, and their various areas of jurisdiction, have not kept pace with changing circumstances. Until the time of the civil war progress towards a more rational organization was made difficult by the fact that the whole of Lagos outside the city boundary was within the former Western Region, which raised political and financial problems of great complexity. As long ago as 1964 a United Nations team had proposed that the artificial distinction between the City (Federal Government) and the built-up area outside (Western Regional Government) should be terminated, and that a Greater Lagos Metropolitan Authority should operate over the whole conurbation in the manner of the LEDB, and that the then Lagos Town Council should act as a second-tier authority, also over the whole area. The undoubted difficulties which stood in the way of this were removed with the creation of the Lagos State, but at the time of writing the multiplicity of authorities has not been reduced.[3] The Federal Ministry

[3] The Report is awaited, however, of a 'Tribunal of Inquiry' into future reorganization, under the chairmanship of Chief Ogunnaike. It seems likely that planning may become a direct responsibility of the Ministry, working through the two existing planning authorities, the LEDB and Ikeja, and that the functions of planning and development may be separated.

of Lagos Affairs is now superseded by two State ministries —Local Government and Chieftaincy Affairs for general purposes and Works and Planning for planning purposes, located at Ikeja, and the jurisdiction of the City Council and the LEDB remain unchanged. Outside the city boundary —in the territory taken over from the Western Region— urban planning is the responsibility of the Ikeja Planning Authority and there are also four 'divisional' local authorities for general purposes—Ikeja, Badagry, Epe and Ikorodu, the last three of which are still largely rural, but which are of course near enough to the metropolis to feel the influences of urbanization.

We have here the universal problem of the big growing city and its hinterland. The city boundary is always slow to catch up with the real area of the city, which has led in some parts of the world to the growth of what is usually called the 'City Region'—a ring thrown round the city sufficiently widely to anticipate future problems of urban growth and to solve them by a single authority, or at least a co-ordinated set of agencies. Generally speaking, West African governments have not adopted such a *positive* attitude towards town and country planning;[4] the phrase 'town planning' is associated with control rather than with forward strategy, and the State Ministry of Local Government and the City Council alike deal with such matters as the modernizing of markets and abattoirs rather than the strategic location of population and industry and the traffic strategies that these involve.

Ibadan

Although Lagos is the worst example in West Africa of 'megalopolis'—the city running riot with no one able to control it—every other large or growing town has its comparable problems. Their solution in West African circumstances is hindered by the usual formidable restrictions of lack of capital, revenue and skill. Ibadan used to be said

[4] Though the Government of Ghana was 'thinking big' in combining the municipal administration of Accra and Tema.

to be the biggest purely African city on the whole African continent. This is no longer true, for Greater Lagos has probably passed it in population and Ibadan is no longer growing at the same *rate* as several other West African cities. It was always firmly linked sociologically with the farming areas round about it, and emigrants from the further parts of Nigeria probably feel the pull of the more powerful magnet of Lagos. Nevertheless it has inherited problems too formidable for solution in this century. It is a city of a million people, without modern sewerage or drainage and with an almost limitless need for slum clearance, rehousing and replanning. Yet as a local authority it has a revenue of no more than a million pounds—a pound a head—which is ludicrously small to tackle even the fringe of its problems. The World Health Organization has spent some years examining the sewerage and drainage problem and is designing a plan which would be workable if sufficient external resources could be recruited to implement it;[5] even so, the necessary cost of maintenance, in terms both of skill and money, would tax an Ibadan City Council to the limit.

Kaduna and Kano

Kaduna, the old Capital Territory of the Northern Region, must be mentioned in this context because although its estimated population in 1967 was less than 200,000 it happens to be, surprisingly, the fastest growing city in the whole of Nigeria, with an annual growth of 11·2%, which is higher than the actual city of Lagos, though it is a good deal less than the Lagos fringe areas. As Kaduna Capital Territory it had the advantage of more spacious and far-sighted planning than most other West African towns, i.e. the Territory covered a 5-mile radius from the city centre; but so unpredictable is the rate of urban growth that already the city administrators are beginning to feel short of space. The city's will to plan spaciously is shown, however, by the

[5] Master Plan for Wastes Disposal and Drainage: WHO—UN Development Programme: First Report.

commissioning some years ago of an overseas town planner to prepare a *50-year* development plan. This was completed in 1966 and approved in principle in 1970, and work is now in progress on the detail.

In 1953 the population of Kano was 131,000; in 1967 it was estimated at 415,000; today it could well be 600,000 as it is growing at an estimated 8·9% per annum. It is a sprawling, spacious place, an unusual challenge to the town planner and city administrator since physically it is a loose conglomeration of ancient city, modern 'township' and commercial centre, international airport and subsidiary townships. But spacious though it is, in the sense that it stands in an endless plain, it is none the less beginning to experience the usual modern problems of traffic congestion, breakdown of public services and shortage of housing. So far as local administration is concerned it is still a tangle of authorities—the old and powerful Kano NA (now called the Local Government Authority), its subordinate authority for the Old City, the Waje Town Council and the administrative officer in charge of the modern commercial part of the city; but it has long been the intention to draw these together in a more rational kind of organization. As long ago as 1962 a Kano Greater Planning Authority was established under the Town and Country Planning Law, and this was replaced in 1969 by the more effective Metropolitan Planning and Development Board, which has assumed planning powers for the whole of Greater Kano; actual development is a more difficult matter as rights in land, e.g. those of the Emir of Kano himself, are a very complicated matter.

The Gold Coast and Ghana

The argument with which we opened this chapter, namely that local government in big towns has a distinctive character of its own, is supported in an interesting way by the early history of the Gold Coast, for as long ago as *1858* the first Municipal Ordinance gave municipal status to Accra and Cape Coast, with representative membership and the power to tax. It was a short-lived failure, for it had to be repealed in 1861, but it is interesting that in 1869 and again in 1887 the educated people of Cape Coast and Accra petitioned, unsuccessfully, for a return to municipal government. It was not until 1894 that a Town Councils Ordinance found its way back on to the statute book, to be applied to Accra in 1898, to Sekondi in 1904 and to Cape Coast in 1906. We mention these experiments merely from historical interest, because it cannot be said that any of them were successful. People wanted representative municipal government, but they didn't want to pay for it or to assume the personal responsibilities and unpopularity that it could entail. The well-known Governor Sir Gordon Guggisberg also tried in 1924 to revive urban local government, but with equal lack of success.

However, in later years the people of Ghana were forced to take urban local government more seriously by the growth of population, the drft from the bush to the towns, and the neglect of the old town centres which brought problems of slums, sanitation, traffic congestion and the rest, so that elected councils with municipal status became responsible for Kumasi, Tamale, Koforidua and Obuasi, as well as for the coastal cities.

Under the new Constitution, and the Local Administration Act 1971, these former municipalities have temporarily lost their distinctive status, but no doubt this will be restored by the subsidiary legislation for which the Act provides. At the time of writing even Accra is in a kind of constitutional limbo, for although 'Greater Accra' is not constitutionally a ninth Region of Ghana comparable arrangements will have to be made for it. Meanwhile, of course, the combined Accra-Tema City Council keeps the main municipal services going, its responsibilities, in order of financial importance, being public health, transport, primary education and social welfare. In Accra itself Development and Works is in fact the second largest item in the budget, but in newly-built Tema it is not of course an important one. The total estimated revenue in 1970/71 was of the order of £2,232,800 for Accra and £971,630 for 'Tema Branch'.

Freetown

Freetown, however, is the grandfather of West African municipalities, for it was first granted a Royal Charter by King George III of England in 1799, since when it has enjoyed the prestige of having a Mayor and Aldermen. It was created a municipality in a more modern sense by an Ordinance of 1893, and is thus the oldest municipality in Africa. The subsequent history of the municipal council, however, has been neither happy nor distinguished, having been characterized by refusal to pay rates, by dishonesty and corruption, and by inefficiency. After vicissitudes lasting more than fifty years it was re-established under its existing Act in 1948.

The shortcomings of the Freetown City Council exemplify, though possibly in an extreme form, those of all West African municipalities. Like the others, its functions are somewhat limited in comparison with municipalities in Britain, since the Government retains direct responsibility for certain services which are often regarded as municipal, including public health. Nevertheless before its suspension in 1967 its range of activities gave rise to eight committees, municipal trading (principally markets), charity, establishments, health, housing and building, protection, recreational facilities and assessment (of rates). It was divided into seven departments, and employed as principal officers a town clerk, a city treasurer, a town engineer, a water engineer, a fire officer, a valuation officer and an education officer in charge of primary education.[6]

Its basic problem, as in the other cities, has always been lack of money. The amounts it can raise as local revenue,

[6] It was restored through elections held on June 3, 1970. Its maladministration was investigated by the Percy Davies Commission of Inquiry into the Activities of the Freetown City Council from January 1, 1964 to March 23, 1967. The Commission disclosed a deplorable state of affairs and made a number of recommendations for reform.

from property rating, are quite unrelated to the needs of an old, crowded and in part decaying city, and Government has not been generous. Accordingly it cannot compete either with the central government or with private industry or commerce as an employer, so that a city of some importance has to be run with totally inadequate resources. This inherent weakness has been made worse from time to time during the Council's history, and notably in the 1960s, by the stark corruption of the elected councillors, including Mayors.

A problem which is peculiar to Freetown in its exact form, but which is of universal interest in slightly different forms, is that of the rural areas surrounding the city, in what used to be known as the Colony, where there is a special arrangement which derives from the historical development of the country and the needs of the original immigrant 'creole' population. This was embodied in the Rural Areas Ordinance of 1950, and consists of a hierarchy of councils, chosen by indirect election, and comprising village committees, rural district councils and the Rural Areas Council. Considering that some of these areas are now almost 'outer suburban' it seems an anomalous arrangement, reminiscent of some of the historical survivals which have recently been swept away in Britain under the recent reorganization of local government. But the fringes of growing cities frequently set problems of this kind.

Elected councils

During the late 1960s elected councils, city, urban and rural alike, were suspended and replaced either by civil servants or nominated committees of management. At the time of writing a modified form of representative local government is being restored in many places, but the situation changes from month to month and it would be pointless to describe the existing position in any detail.

In very brief summary, therefore, the Freetown City Council has, as we have already mentioned, been once more elected; it comprises a mayor, three aldermen and nine elected councillors, one alderman and three councillors being elected in each of three wards, with the addition of six nominated members. In Lagos the Government's Sole Administrator has been replaced by a 'caretaker committee' of 36 members, which however has already been reproved by the Military Governor for neglect of duty. Ibadan, on the other hand, has no representative body, but is in charge of a Government Administrator working in conjunction with the Secretary to the former Council. Kano also is administered from the State Military Governor's Office, but Accra-Tema has again become the responsibility of an elected council.

The general picture

We have briefly discussed the position in half a dozen of the best-known cities by way of illustration, but comparable situations exist in many different places; for example, in the cosmopolitan town of Port Harcourt, the Ibo town of Onitsha, in Benin, in the Yoruba towns of Oshogbo, Ife, Iwo, Abeokuta or Ilesha, or in the Ashanti capital of Kumasi. In these, and indeed in smaller places, minimum standards must be maintained and enforced in matters which are less urgent and troublesome in the villages and the bush.

English-speaking West Africa was less fortunate in her urban colonial heritage than other African countries who experienced French, Belgian and German colonial rule. The Continental colonial powers cared more about town and city development than did the British, whose heart was in the bush and among the peasants. Citizens of Freetown, Lagos or Ibadan have only to visit the capitals of their French-speaking neighbours—or even their smaller towns —to see that the French took more care than the British in the lay-out of town centres, the planting of trees and parks, the general amenities of an urban civilization. Nevertheless, although they displayed less imagination than their European rivals, the British did not by any means neglect the problem of urban administration, and for a hundred years before their final departure they distinguished 'municipalities' and various grades of 'township' from the rest of the country and devised special forms of administration for them.[7]

We have already mentioned the older municipalities, some of them dating from the nineteenth century. Almost all of them were on the coast (Kumasi being an exception), and were cosmopolitan places, with a mixture of races and with overseas interests. But there were in addition smaller towns classed as 'Townships'—in Nigeria as First, Second and Third Class Townships. Some had Advisory Boards, on which local elected representatives made their first appearance; others were virtually administered by a District Officer, who came to be known by the confusing name of *'the* Local Authority' a description which still persists in, for example, the Township area of Greater Kano. Obuasi in Ashanti was administered until 1952 by a so-called Sanitary Board, on which the Ashanti Goldfields Corporation was represented.[8]

These are now matters of history, and as far as details are concerned they have nothing more than an historical interest. But a general proposition survives, namely that when towns reach a certain size local government begins to assume a new character and a greater urgency. This is even truer of West Africa than of Britain, Germany or America, where the gap between the urban and rural mode of life has narrowed. In Britain, for example, one of the objects of current local government reform is to abolish what has now become an artificial distinction between town and country, since the two are increasingly inter-

---

[7] *Native Administration in the British African Territories* (Part III—West Africa) by Lord Hailey, is a comprehensive description of what we should now call local government immediately after the Second World War. The various sections headed 'The Municipalities' or 'The Urban Areas' bear out what is said here.

[8] 'Company' local government, where a locality is dominated by a large mining, plantation or other industrial concern, is often to be found in the developing world, where the resources of the Company exceed those of the Government.

dependent and merge into one another, and rural living standards are as high as urban ones. But in most of rural Africa standards in such things as housing, sanitation, minor roads and public amenities are of the simplest, and the tasks to which a village or rural council has to put its hand have little in common with those of a town or city council. Still less is there any affinity in their organization and procedures. City government throughout the world is becoming more managerial, more mechanized, more streamlined, and some of the larger cities of West Africa are beginning to think in terms of the scientific management of their business. But the task of rural local government is community development, meaning by that very versatile phrase self-help and neighbourly co-operation directed towards simple material improvement.

Having grouped together the towns of Sierra Leone, Ghana and Nigeria for the purposes of this chapter, let us now examine each country in turn with reference to the local government pattern outside the towns.

CHAPTER 9

Sierra Leone

AT the time of writing local government in Sierra Leone is in a state of suspended animation, awaiting a report of a *Committee on the Review of Local Government Structure in Sierra Leone*. It was appointed in 1969. Two years earlier a Local Government (Miscellaneous Provisions) Act had empowered the Government to suspend any elected council and to replace it for six months with a committee of management, a power which was comprehensively used. In this chapter we examine the working of the system which is currently under review.

It is well worth examining, irrespective of its shortcomings, since unlike the systems in Ghana and Southern Nigeria it owes nothing to British or any other foreign legislation. It grew out of traditional forms of local administration, supplemented by a piece of machinery designed to implement a Development Plan at district level. The pattern of local administration outside Freetown and a few Townships comprises: 147 'chiefdoms', 12 'districts', 3 'provinces'.

The Chiefdoms

The paramount chiefs are the traditional agents of local administration, and the chiefdoms are still the base of the local government pyramid, and are fundamental to the government of the country, though the prestige of the chiefs suffered a considerable blow in the years 1954 and 1955. This arose partly from the fact that with the stirrings of nationalism in the early 1950s, but without any legislative changes in the system of local government, the powers of the expatriate district commissioners were considerably reduced, and their rôle altered from the executive to the advisory. This was somewhat premature, for a number of chiefs, removed from the firm control of the DC, started to behave badly and to use their powers for personal extortion. There were widespread riots against them, resulting in a Commission of Enquiry from whose Report they emerged with little credit.[1] In the years since then, however, they have done much to recover their position.

Chiefdoms are established under an Ordinance of 1938 known as the Tribal Authorities Ordinance, and the correct name for what elsewhere would be known as the council is in fact the 'tribal authority', though they are customarily referred to as 'native administrations'; the tribal authority, in the words of the Ordinance, means 'the paramount chief, the chiefs, the councillors and men of note elected by the people according to native law and custom, approved by the Governor', and generally numbers between forty and sixty members. Local government in Sierra Leone is therefore based on traditional bodies and not, as in Ghana and Southern Nigeria, on councils predominantly elected by secret ballot.

As organs of local government the tribal authorities have been neither representative nor efficient; their meetings have been infrequent, often no more than twice a year, their government autocratic and in the hands of ruling cliques, and the powers of the chiefs arbitrary. These facts have been recognized by the Government since 1954 by their encouragement—administratively and not by legislation— of 'chiefdom councils' and 'chiefdom committees'. The former were intended to make the tribal authorities more representative, by compelling them to take into consultation both the chiefdom members on the district council (see below, p. 158) and a number of members (specifically

[1] Report of a Commission of Enquiry into Disturbances in the Provinces, November 1955 to March 1956 (published by the Crown Agents on behalf of the Government of Sierra Leone).

to include young men) who would be elected by taxpayers from the different sections of the chiefdom. The chiefdom committees were intended to make them more efficient by appointing the more literate and able members of the tribal authority, together with others, to form a kind of standing Finance and General Purposes Committee which would keep the business affairs of the authority under constant review. Neither councils nor committees have operated with any system or uniformity throughout the country, but they have to some extent modernized the tribal authorities and brought them closer to the realities of twentieth-century administration.

The position of the chief himself is not easy to define, and has more in common with that of chiefs in Uganda and other parts of East and Central Africa than of the paramount chiefs of Ghana or the obas of Western Nigeria. On the one hand, he is chosen by traditional methods and his office carries, on proper occasions, the ceremony and dignity associated with traditional chieftainship; on the other hand for most of his working life he more resembles a hard-working local government officer or civil servant, as he is the principal executive officer of the tribal authority, working each day in authority's office, and the effectiveness of the authority depends to a great extent on his ability. He is in fact in the rather invidious position, like 'executive' chiefs in many other parts of Africa, of being part natural local ruler, part local government official and part civil servant.[2] However, there is no doubt about his importance in the general scheme of government; it is said that in the early days of the nationalists' demand for self-government Nkrumah in Ghana appealed to the people for support but in Sierra Leone Sir Milton Margai appealed to the chiefs.

[2] The word 'chief' as used in English-speaking Africa is one of the most unsatisfactory words in the English language, as it has been used to describe, in a legal sense, everything from a king, as in Ashanti or Buganda, to a minor civil servant wearing uniform, as in Kenya.

As local government units the chiefdoms are small, and their work considerably more restricted than that of local councils in other parts of West Africa. On a very rough average they cover the area occupied by about 3,000 adult male taxpayers, a good deal more in the industrial areas where iron ore and diamonds are mined (e.g. close on 6,000 in Port Loko District), and a good deal less in the poorer and more rural areas (e.g. about 1,800 in Pujehun District). Their principal activity is still the native court,[3] which in the other coastal territories has been gradually separated from the work of the local councils. The paramount chief, however, is not the court president, who is now elected by the tribal authority; the separation of the chief from the court was made to remove doubts about the impartiality of the president, and to this extent a beginning has been made with distinguishing between executive and judicial functions. These courts are, as elsewhere, largely occupied with such matters as dowry, debt, inheritance, land, etc., and in certifying cases of theft or violence to the magistrates' court. In other words the chief activity of the tribal authorities lies in discharging their responsibility for 'order and good government' and the 'prevention of crime'.

This, however, is by no means the end of their potential responsibilities. Their powers and duties under the Ordinance are not dissimilar from those of local authorities elsewhere, but because of their restricted means they are carried out in a more modest fashion. They may 'issue orders' on such matters as water pollution, burning-off, cultivation, the movement of livestock and may control nuisances. They may also make by-laws, subject to the usual approvals, on the normal range of activities of small local authorities such as markets, slaughter houses, wash places, the sale of food and drink, street trading, fees, licences and building

[3] By an Act of 1963 the native courts have been re-named 'local courts', their area of jurisdiction, both in civil and criminal cases, has been extended, and they have been brought into the normal appelate system of the country.

lines. An interesting point is that orders and by-laws must be 'orally promulgated', i.e. publicly announced, as well as being 'posted in the court barri or market place of the principal town of the chiefdom'.

The chiefdoms also make small contributions to education, medical and health services, agriculture, forestry and roads, though the main responsibility for these falls on the higher 'District Councils' or on the provincial departments of the central government. In the case of roads the contribution may take the form of communal labour to maintain minor roads rather than of financial expenditure.

Finally, the chiefdom is the tax assessment and tax collecting authority, a point which will be discussed a little later in dealing with their revenue.

The chiefdoms are strictly controlled by higher authority, and have never been given the freedom which was at one time given to the local authorities in Eastern Nigeria, or is at present given to the 'financially autonomous' councils of Western Nigeria. A higher authority must approve most of the things they do, including their budgeting, and may compel them to do things which they are failing to do. The 'higher authority' was in colonial days the (Provincial) Chief Commissioner and the Governor, but their powers have now become vested in the Provincial Resident Minister.

The tribal authorities of Sierra Leone used to budget for sums varying from Le 10,000 to Le 30,000, and a typical budget might have read like this:

1.	Precept to District Council	6,000
2.	Hereditary officials	5,500
3.	Administration	2,000
4.	Native Court	3,000
5.	Messengers	3,000
6.	Prison	400
7.	Education	750
8.	Medical and Health	2,000
9.	Agriculture	300

10. Forestry	1,200
11. Works	1,000
12. Miscellaneous	2,000
	27,150

The first and largest item is of particular interest. The finances of the district councils, which we will discuss in a moment, rested largely on the 'precept', which as we said on p. 62 has been largely unsuccessful elsewhere in Africa; but in this instance it has worked reasonably well. Human nature being what it is, there has been the usual grumbling in the chiefdoms at having to pass so much money over to the districts, and complaints that they wasted it, but in practice it has been paid without undue difficulty. It represented something like one leone per head out of a total individual tax of $2\frac{1}{2}$ leones.

The money spent on education was for local scholarships in the form of half fees for chiefdom children in secondary schools; on agriculture, to pay a man in charge of a seedling nursery; on forestry, for paying forest guards; and on works, for food and customary 'dashes' for communal labour supplied to the district council for unskilled road work—a sensible and economical way of getting public work done.

The revenue of the same council might have been made up as follows:

1. Local tax (6,000 at Le $2\frac{1}{2}$)	15,000
2. Court receipts	6,200
3. Grants from central government for administration	3,000
4. Miscellaneous	300
5. Licences	600
6. Fees	50
7. Markets and lorry parks	2,000
	27,150

With regard to item 3 it was the practice of Government to pay direct to the chiefdoms 50% of the remuneration of the paramount chief, the clerks and the messengers.

Since the chiefdoms are the tax assessment and collecting authorities, it will be appropriate to say something at this point about local taxation (the word 'rate' is not used except in connection with the property rate in the townships). This is controlled by the Local Tax Ordinance of 1955, which prescribes that every male over twenty-one shall be liable to pay tax (as compared with sixteen in Ghana and eighteen in Nigeria). Tax assessment committees are appointed by the tribal authority to determine the amount of the tax each year. There is no graduated tax apart from the central government income tax, which does not apply to incomes under £300 a year, and which is only just beginning to be levied outside the main urban centres of population; in most of the chiefdoms £300 a year would be far above the level of income of the vast majority of people. The tax is normally payable to a chief or headman, who receives a commission, but employers of labour may be appointed by the Minister to collect the tax from their employees.

District councils

Although the name 'district council' is a familiar one, there is in fact nothing to correspond to the Sierra Leone district councils in the other West African countries. This is because they were not originally intended only—or even primarily—as organs of local government, though the possibility of this development was foreshadowed. They were in the first place simply groupings of chiefdoms through which the Government intended to channel a certain proportion of the funds voted for development under a Development Plan of 1949.[4] This in itself could have been a sound and encouraging basis on which to reform and modernize local government, since the weakness in Southern Nigeria and Ghana was that a somewhat elaborate structure of local government had been erected without very much inside it; that is to say, there has been a hierarchy of

[4] The Childs Report on Economic Development in Sierra Leone, 1949.

councils with extensive powers on paper, but with little opportunity to exercise those powers because of the lack of funds. To bring a new type of authority into being for the specific purpose of spending money on development—money which would be provided by the central government and the Produce Marketing Board—could have brought a greater sense of reality to local government than elsewhere.

This point of view is summed up in the Childs Report itself:[5]

> 'At the end of 1949 the Government decided to devolve much of its plan of economic development on to districts. The resources . . . would be pooled in district councils. . . . This decision offered an opportunity not only for developing the internal economy . . . but also for an important step forward in the organization of local government. . . . The criticism that local government bodies have sometimes been set up as an administrative exercise without any clear idea of what they can do can certainly not be levelled at this measure. Councils were established because there was a practical job to be done and an organization required to do it.'

The venture was only partly successful. It is true that from 1951 to 1956, at first under the chairmanship of the district commissioner and from 1954 under a president appointed by the Governor in Council, the district councils fulfilled the rôle allotted to them, among other things spending grants on agricultural improvements as a contribution to the wider development plan. From the point of view of building a new kind of local authority, however, there was one serious weakness, namely that the district councils were not fulfilling the rôle of local authorities but were simply doing local agency work for the central government, spending, under direction, sums of money provided for specific purposes. This may have been useful,

[5] Quoted in the Report of the Commission of Enquiry into Disturbances in the Provinces, op. cit.

but it was not a proper training for local democracy, and the removal of the district commissioners as chairmen in 1954 did not add even to their usefulness, as the presidents who took their place interfered, in a manner all too familiar in Nigeria and Ghana, with the secretary and staff in the execution of their duties.

However, the intention to build them up into new multi-purpose local authorities was followed, and was embodied in the District Councils (Amendment) Ordinance of 1954. This Ordinance, which was the one which removed the district commissioners from the chairmanships, also introduced the precept on the chiefdoms as a new source of revenue to supplement the Government grant, extended their range of functions, and slightly altered their membership. It was the Ordinance under which the councils were operating at the time of their suspension.

Each district was divided into 'wards', based very roughly on 1,000 taxpayers; since chiefdoms vary from about 2,000 to 6,000 taxpayers, it follows that there will be several wards in each chiefdom. The district council then consists of the chief, one member elected from each ward, *the local members of the legislative council* (another interesting departure from the usual practice elsewhere) and a few co-opted members. A full district council could have numbered some sixty to eighty members, which raises the question of what is a workable size for an effective council in local government. Certainly this is too large in the circumstances of West Africa, which is borne out by the fact that few district councils met more often than the statutory minimum, which was twice a year; even this could have cost Le 2,000 a year—a very large sum in relative terms—merely in paying for councillors' travelling expenses and sitting fees. It follows from this that the council itself was not an effective body for transacting business, but had more of the character of a local parliament, in which there was very little restriction on the subjects which appear to have no relation to the work of local government were raised and debated. Meetings of this kind have, of course, considerable value, and one particularly useful feature of them is that they provide technical officers of the Government, or indeed eminent visitors to the country, with an opportunity to address a representative audience on matters of importance.

The more serious and regular work of the council, however, was effectively done by the Finance and General Purposes Committee, and a few other committees, which met monthly.

District councils are expected to provide their own secretary, treasurer, works supervisor and subordinate staff, but in most districts there are central or provincial government 'assigned' staff; that is to say education, health, agricultural and forestry officers who are assigned to work in the district. An assigned officer is not, however, the same thing as a seconded officer, for he continues to be employed by the Government, which pays his salary.

When we come to consider the functions of district councils, we find another interesting variation from the British-type legislation adopted in Ghana and Southern Nigeria. Such legislation was, as we have seen, governed by the doctrine of *ultra vires*, which restricts local authorities to doing only those things which the law specifically entitles them to do. The functions of the district councils are cast in much more general terms; their purpose is:

(1) To promote the development of the District and the welfare of the people with the funds at its disposal.

(2) To advise on any matter brought before it by direction of the Minister.

(3) To make recommendations to the Government on matters affecting the welfare of the people as a whole.

On paper, therefore, the district councils were free to go ahead with development of any kind. In practice their work was extremely restricted, and consisted almost entirely of building and maintaining roads and primary schools. It has to be remembered that in communications especially Sierra Leone is some years behind Ghana and Nigeria, and that for the foreseeable future the energies of district councils and tribal authorities alike could be largely absorbed in the most fundamental of all development work, i.e. joining villages together by road and thus enabling farmers to get their produce out of the bush and into the market. Even so and in spite of the fact that these are the most important tasks of the district councils, only about half of them were able to employ a qualified works superintendent or to maintain a reasonably well equipped works yard. Apart from the construction of simple bridges and culverts, road building is still largely a matter of pick, shovel and 'elbow grease'. Lack of funds and lack of skilled employees kept the district councils' work within these modest limits.

The expenditure of a typical district council before the suspension of the elected members might have been in the neighbourhood of Le 120,000, of which about Le 25,000 might have been spent on school building, Le 15,000 on school maintenance and Le 35,000 on roads. The balance would have been spent on minor projects connected with agriculture, forestry and public health. The revenue of such a council would have come in roughly equal proportions from three sources:

Grants for specific development projects
Ordinary grants in aid
Contributions from chiefdoms

In other words grant aid from the Government would have accounted for two thirds of the revenue, and the precept from the chiefdoms for a third.

The Townships

Outside the capital city of Freetown there are very few towns of any considerable size, the largest being Bo, Kenema and Makeni, the three provincial capitals, and the rapidly growing iron ore town of Marampa-Lunsar. Bo has been a township for a considerable time, under a special Bo Town Council Ordinance, but the government of towns has now been regularized by the Townships Ordinance of 1959, and Kenema and Makeni are now governed by its provisions.

The Ordinance provides that the membership of a town council shall comprise a president, who shall be the paramount chief of the chiefdom in which the town is situated, two councillors elected from each ward, two members nominated by the Resident Minister and two members appointed by the local tribal authority. A chairman (as distinct from the president) is elected annually, all members hold office for four years, and qualifications include literacy in English. Councils are expected to appoint a town clerk, treasurer, medical officer of health, surveyor and bailiff, though their appointment and dismissal are subject to Ministerial approval. In practice, because of the shortage of qualified men, the minister of health and the surveyor are more likely to be provincial officers devoting part of their time to the affairs of the town council.

The powers and duties of the town councils follow the usual lines; their mandatory duties involve sanitation and the upkeep of roads, streets, culverts, markets, slaughter houses and cemeteries; their permissive powers include such things as planning and layouts, lighting, fire precautions and washing and bathing places; they may also impose licence fees on traders, hotels and lodging houses, money lenders, sellers of palm wine and patent medicines, and also on vehicles, other than motor vehicles. They have also the more controversial power, which does not appear in all types of local government law, of engaging 'with the approval of the Minister . . . in any form of public undertaking, trading or industry.

The failure of the District Councils

In theory, the system we have just described has a great deal to be said for it. It recognizes the strength of ancient custom but tries to harness it to modern purposes, and it gives the basic local government unit money to spend on development. Yet it has not succeeded, and from about

1965 it has been marking time or slipping back.[6] The failure has largely been at district level, as may be seen from the following Private Member's motion to Parliament in January 1969:

> That in view of the terrible waste of public funds by about 90% of the District Councils in the last seven years running into hundreds of thousands of leones and in view of the lack of competent staff to man the running of these bodies, be it resolved that the Government gives serious consideration as to whether District Councils shall continue to function.

It was this motion that launched the Committee on the Review of the Local Government System to which we referred in the first sentence of this chapter, under the chairmanship of the Minister of Finance.[7] There were a number of reasons for the failure and it is difficult to say that one was more important than another. There was much corruption and waste, which resulted in the chiefdoms becoming more and more reluctant to pay their precepts. It may well be that irresponsibility was encouraged by the fact that district councillors did not have to raise any money themselves, which would have made them accountable to taxpayers, but received it either from the Government above or the chiefdoms below. But perhaps most fundamentally there were insufficient resources (in 'competent staff' as much as in money) to service three different 'agencies' of development—Province, District and Chiefdom. The Government provincial staffs had most of the resources and the chiefdoms were closest to the people.

---

[6] It did not completely fail or collapse. Precepts paid by chiefdoms rose from Le 1,206,000 in 1962 to 1,575,000 in 1968, and district council estimates were over a million leones in 1969/70 compared with 913,000 in the previous year. But this is a mere standstill, or even retreat, if inflation is allowed for, and tax collection started to fall into arrears, and never recovered, from 1965 onwards.

[7] The chairman of a Working Committee was a United Nations Consultant from the Economic Commission for Africa.

In between the two, district councils had to justify their existence, and this they failed to do. Certainly when the Review Committee was appointed the morale of the district staffs was low and their achievements at a standstill. Whether they are to be abolished or strengthened—which broadly speaking are the alternatives—should be known by the time this book appears in print. The most likely move is away from 'local government' and towards 'local administration'.

CHAPTER 10

Ghana

'NATIVE ADMINISTRATION' throughout British West Africa first began to be modernized as a result of a directive from the Secretary of State for the Colonies in the post-War Labour Government, to the Governors of African colonies, that they should work towards the establishment of 'efficient and representative local government'. In the Gold Coast the trend was quickened by the after-effects of the riots of 1948, and notably by the proposals of the all-African Committee on Constitutional Reform presided over by the late Sir Henley Coussey. In the light of hindsight we can see that their plans to modernize native administration were unduly influenced by the British model of local government,[1] just as parliamentary reform was to be unduly influenced by Westminster. Nevertheless a start had to be made somewhere, and it is understandable that they should have wanted to break away from the colonial hierarchy, which was French rather than British in character, and from a form of local government which, outside the towns, substantially meant the chiefs and their 'state' councils. The Committee's ideas were to be embodied in the first Local Government Ordinance of 1951, which adopted the three-tier English system, including the device of precepting, and reduced the chiefs and their followers to a minority among an elected majority. It was, however, a

---

[1] '. . . we have attempted, in effect, to achieve a synthesis of the traditional type of local government in this country with the more developed democratic form of local government in the United Kingdom, which, after careful consideration, we have taken as our model rather than that of either France or America.'

largely political exercise, for although the new councils were more 'representative' they were certainly no more 'efficient', since their resources were no greater than those of the native authorities they succeeded. The system was also far too complicated.

By 1956 its failure was openly admitted, and a Commissioner, Mr. A. F. Greenwood, was appointed to extricate local government from the morass into which it had fallen. The Greenwood Report is still worth reading, for although it has now passed into history the problems it faced and its suggestions for tackling them have a contemporary ring.

The 1951 Act had established 26 upper-tier authorities ('districts') and 252 lower-tier ('local' and 'urban'). Thirty-one of the latter had populations under 5,000, the smallest being less than 1,000; 75 had populations between 5,000 and 10,000.

> 'Many of these small councils are surviving only by virtue of Government or Cocoa Marketing Board grants—others are capable of carrying on at their present level of activity but with little hope of making progress. The ability to survive is not enough.'

It was at once apparent to the Commissioner that there was no hope of persuading councils to overcome their difficulties by amalgamating; on the contrary, as soon as the possibility of change was discussed the general desire was to fragment still further, and to revert to the even smaller petty chiefdoms which the 1951 Act had done something to reduce. He accordingly had to leave the small units as they were, but to recommend the transfer of their powers and functions to some larger body which had some chance of actually exercising them—leaving the local and urban councils as the equivalent of English parishes, without staff or funds. This was in fact the proposal that was accepted in principle—that the 26 district councils should have become the effective units of local government.

It is worth noting in passing that he put up an alternative proposal, rejected by the Government, which was certainly more interesting and adventurous. The country was at that time divided into six Regions—the present number is eight—which were an administrative heritage from colonial days, and whose headquarters controlled the best technical skill and equipment in the country (as did the three Sierra Leone Provinces), e.g. in public works, education, health, agriculture and forestry. The proposal was that each Region should become the effective local authority for major services, leaving the 252 lower councils with minor powers and rating functions, but giving them an incentive to combine by offering increased functions with increased population, e.g. councils of a suggested minimum of 20,000 would control only primary education and local water supplies; but between 20,000 and 30,000 clinics and dispensaries would be added, and up to 50,000 middle education and the maintenance of minor roads.

This alternative had its attractions, partly because to have identified the Regional authority with local government would have given local government greater prestige in the eyes of the people, and partly because it would have been interesting to see whether the appeal of greater modern powers and duties would have been stronger or weaker than the pull of traditional chieftainship and local rivalry.

Unfortunately the resulting legislation, which was to be consolidated in the Local Government Act 1961, did neither one thing nor the other, but simply produced a compromise which made the worst of both worlds. The Commissioner had recommended 26 districts; the Act established 104. He recommended that local and small urban councils should have neither staff nor funds; but over 150 remained with both. The Ghana Government of the day allowed itself to be swayed by local lobbies and pressures, especially as it became clear that the popularity of the Party depended on local concessions being made. It must, of course, be remembered that this was the Government of Nkrumah in 1961, and by this time all pretence that local government was anything but an extension of the Party had been virtually abandoned.

Along with the Local Government Law 1961 the Government passed the Chiefs' Law, which gave statutory recognition to the chiefs' ceremonial and traditional functions, but banished them for ever (as it then seemed) from the administration of local government.

It will be seen in a moment that this digression into the 1961 Laws, and the events which led up to them, has a very direct relevance to the circumstances surrounding the Local Administration Act *1971*, which is beginning to be implemented at the time of writing.

The Law of 1961 to the Coup of 1966

Some time before the Law of 1961 local government in Ghana had in fact cast off its English garments and assumed those of pseudo-communism. Elections in local government had been abandoned in 1959, though the formality of 'unopposed' elections continued. These were in effect compulsory votes of confidence in the Party, since the electorate had no choice but to vote for a Party list, drawn up by the local Party organizer. Council secretaries were Party men, and one of the functions of the local Party organizer was to see that councillors were properly versed in the ideology of Nkrumahism, and to discipline or dismiss them if they were recalcitrant.

During these years the Nkrumah Government did in fact dilute the functions of the councils by placing some of them elsewhere and reviving town and village committees, which although surrounded by much improving propaganda about 'grass-roots development' were in the opinion of detached observers little more than an excuse to withdraw government grant-aid from local government, which was becoming necessary because of the country's approaching bankruptcy.

The Department of Community Development

Before discussing the re-emergence of local government

with the 1970 Constitution and the return of civilian rule, a word must be said about the relationship between local government and community development. This is a general problem, which perhaps ought to be dealt with in one of the more general chapters of this book, but its incidence in Ghana was particularly acute throughout the 1950s and 1960s.

However community development is defined—and the definitions have been many and various—its ultimate purpose, especially in rural areas, is similar to that of local government. It uses different means—for example it needs more informality and less bureaucracy; it requires younger people than those who are normally elected to local councils, and it needs more women; it relies on the active participation of all instead of delegation or responsibility to a few. These are large differences, but since the ultimate objectives are the same[2] it is clear that there ought to be close collaboration between Departments of Community Development and of Local Government. Indeed it has been said[3] that local government ought to be the framework and community development the content, and that the permanent statutory existence of local councils and their power to raise money by local taxes ought to complement the enthusiasm and self-help of community development teams. Community development is good at initiating projects, such as roads or maternity centres, but not so good at maintaining them when they fall into disrepair.

In Ghana the Department of Community Development has always been unusually strong, with substantial funds from Government and with able and inspiring leadership. It has not, however, worked in close contact with the

[2] Compare, for example, the work of the community development teams in Ghana with the powers and duties of local councils as stated in the Local Government Ordinance 1951 and the Law of 1961. They are almost identical.

[3] By Sir Andrew Cohen, who was largely responsible for the post-war local government and community development policies of the British Colonial Office in the years before political independence.

Local Government Department, to whom it has accordingly seemed at times to be a more powerfully equipped rival. For example, community development teams with lorries, publicity apparatus, machinery for making roads or sinking wells have conducted intensive campaigns with great success, but have caused the efforts of the local council, with one works foreman and a 'shoe-string' budget, to seem feeble in the extreme.

The 1970 Constitution

The rehabilitation of local government by the National Liberation Council was the subject of extraordinarily detailed investigation and discussion. Three documents paved the way towards the Act which now prevails—the *Report of the Committee on the Structure and Remuneration of the Public Service in Ghana* (usually known as the Mills-Odoi Report), the *Commission of Enquiry into Electoral and Local Government Reform* (usually known as the Siriboe Commission), and finally Chapter Sixteen (Chieftaincy and Local Government) of the 1970 *Constitution of the Republic of Ghana*.

The Mills-Odoi Report, which was published in December 1967, was largely concerned with examining what then existed on the ground, though in terms of broad principle it made some proposals for the future. It found that local government and everything connected with it was on the verge of 'complete collapse' (paragraph 27). One of the early acts of the NLC had been to banish the elected councillor, and under Decree No. 26 of 1966 they had substituted small nominated committees of management comprising a few local departmental heads with the District Administrative Officer in charge; in 1969 Decree No. 229 established larger committees, retaining three departmental heads but admitting three traditional and ten 'other' members, who were usually professional men, traders or retired officials. The phrase 'complete collapse' was no doubt justified by the personal record of the councillors, by the fact that local government expenditure was far exceeding revenue and by the mounting sums of irrecoverable unpaid rates and taxes. On the other hand it is interesting to note that in spite of the surrounding chaos the 1969–70 revenue of all local authorities was Nc 10 million, compared with Nc 5½ million in 1962–63. The collapse was never complete, and in the latter years of the 1961 Local Government Law the staffs and committees of management of the old local authorities managed to save something from the wreck. The Mills-Odoi Report in making some general recommendations for the future was obviously impressed by the 'managerial' systems of local government which are to be found in some parts of the world, and on which stress is being laid in contemporary Britain. They saw the best hope for the future, in professional management—in, so to speak, a chairman and managing director of a council's business.

The Report of the Siriboe Commission,[4] Part III of which was concerned with local government, is the most searching examination of the subject since the Greenwood Commission, to which it refers at a number of points. Like the Greenwood Report it is likely to be of permanent value to the student of the subject, since it is based on a study both of historical principles and of their application in the Gold Coast and Ghana. In the space available an attempt to summarize its contents would be impracticable. It must suffice to say that it discusses in a Ghanaian context virtually all the matters that were discussed in more general terms in Part I of this book.

The Mills-Odoi and Siriboe Reports, and the White Papers that they generated, were digested into the Constitution of the Republic, published in September 1969, and so far as local government is concerned they were distilled into Chapter 16. It is unusual for the written constitution of a country to make such detailed provision for local government, which is normally a matter for departmental legislation. To enshrine it in the Constitution gives it exceptional prestige, and suggests that it is more than

[4] Accra Government Printer, 1968, Part III.

an ordinary piece of governmental machinery; that it is the embodiment of something more fundamental—almost an expression of human rights and duties. It is important also in that it finally integrates 'regional' and 'local' government. Historically regional administration was associated with the central Government and local administration with the native authorities and their successors. In a relatively small country like Ghana, in an age of improving communications, this integration represents a progressive step, the possibility of which was foreshadowed in the Greenwood Report of 1957; though the regional function in Ghana today is one of strategic planning rather than the administration of services.

Chapter 16 deals with Chieftaincy as well as Local Government, and begins by establishing a National House of Chiefs with appellate jurisdiction in all chieftaincy matters and the duty to undertake the study and codification of systems of customary law. Below them are Regional Houses with both original and appellate jurisdiction.

Proceeding to local government, the Constitution establishes Local, District and Regional Councils (the last-named under the general heading of 'Local Government Councils') and goes into some detail as to their membership. These membership provisions contain a number of points of interest. In the first place they restore to the chiefs their place in local government from which they were ejected in 1961. In local councils it is possible for half the members to be 'traditional', in district councils a third, and in regional councils there are to be two members of the Regional House of Chiefs. Second, the regional councils, although categorized as local government councils, are to include as members, without voting rights, the regional heads of Ministries (provided they do not exceed half the total number), and the chairman is to be appointed by the Prime Minister. Third, the principle of indirect election, which has largely fallen into disfavour, is restored at the regional level, since members are to be elected by *district councils.*

The Constitution briefly indicates the functions of the three types of council, but only in general terms, leaving them to be more precisely defined by legislation. In the matter of membership, however, little discretion is left to subsequent legislation.

Perhaps even more unusual, the Constitution itself (paragraph 160) states that the Government shall make grants-in-aid to regional, district and local councils, the determination of which is to be made, and reviewed at not less than five-yearly intervals, by a Local Government Grants Commission, the membership of which is specified in some detail. This is clearly an insurance against a repetition of the events of the 1960s, when many local councils were so starved of resources that their functions, and indeed their purpose, became somewhat nominal.

The Local Administration Act 1971

This Act fills in the details of the constitutional provisions, in relation to the functions and the machinery of the regional, district and local councils. It is an attempt to find the proper balance between a system of quasi-autonomous elected councils, which had proved so disastrous in many parts of Africa in the past, and straightforward administration by agencies of Government, which would probably not have been tolerated by the Ghanaian people or their representatives in Parliament. It proved to be contentious, many critics believing that it weighted the scales too much in favour of the central government and relegated local government councils to the status of their agents. It was, however, the Government's stated intention to integrate the two more closely than in the past, and in view of the record of local government councillors it was surely a reasonable intention. Indeed, one of the more significant things about the Act was that it was called the Local Administration, and not the Local Government, Act. The change of name was indicative of a new departure in thinking.

The Regional Councils

As we have seen, the Constitution was so specific about regional councils that there was little for the Act to do but translate its intentions into legislative form. It is primarily a planning body, concerned with development plans and programmes; it must of course approve, co-ordinate and supervise the development programmes of the constituent districts, and is charged with the allocation of public funds to district councils on behalf of the Local Government Grants Commission. Since a regional council is so widely representative, comprising elected councillors, chiefs and professional officers, and since its function is in essence the determination of plans and priorities, it is appropriate that its chairman should be a direct representative of the central government, i.e. a nominee of the Prime Minister. In the last resort he has a political function.

The Act goes further than the Constitution, however, by giving the chairman the additional title of Regional Chief Executive, thus adopting at regional level the managerial proposals of the Mills-Odoi Report. Moreover in a clause sub-titled 'Regional Management' provision is made for a Regional Administrative Officer, i.e. a civil servant, who stands to the Regional Chief Executive in the relationship of Principal Secretary to Minister.

The District Councils

The Memorandum to the Local Administration Bill said of the district councils that they would be

'... the fundamental local government unit, with a strong staff, carrying out most of the functions of government which are capable of being exercised at District level.'

They are likely to number between forty and fifty (compared with the twenty-six councils bearing the same name in the 1951 Local Government Ordinance) and they will probably comprise between 18 and 24 members. In the first draft of the Bill it was proposed that the two-thirds majority should be elected indirectly, by a 'District Electoral College' of all the local council members in the district, but this was dropped and it was left to the Electoral Commissioner to make regulations.

The functions of district councils are stated in the broadest possible terms to be

> '... the administration and development of the area of its authority and the provision of public services in that area',

but these somewhat vague and general purposes may be supplemented by 'other functions *not excluding commercial activities*' which the Minister may specify by Instrument.

But the most contentious part of the Local Administration Act was, without question, the extent to which the district council was to become part of the deconcentration of the central Government and to be brought under the authority of its appointees. Not only was it, in the discharge of its functions, to be subject to the 'general guidance and direction' of Ministers acting through regional councils, but its chairman was to be appointed by the Prime Minister, and a civil servant—the District Administrative Officer—was, as one of his duties, to be its secretary. His other duties are those of the local representative of the central government in the fullest sense—the supervision, direction and implementation of the day-to-day functions of all Ministries and Departments within his district. In other words he is a man of the authority of a District Commissioner in colonial days or of a *sous-préfet* in French administration.

We have argued that the chairman of a regional council, having a broadly political function, may appropriately be appointed by the Prime Minister, but this method of appointment may seem somewhat incongruous to the chairmanship of the 'fundamental local government unit'. The same is true of the administrative officer as its secretary. A council which may neither elect its chairman nor appoint its secretary comes close to being part of the apparatus of central government.

The Local Councils

Local councils are somewhat cursorily dealt with both by the Constitution and the Act, which devotes a single clause to them and assigns them the somewhat nebulous rôle of assisting the district council, particularly in rate collection, and performing any tasks that it may delegate. The Memorandum to the Bill was somewhat more informative, since it said that they 'will essentially be community development authorities'. This seems to be their natural rôle, and to accord with the fact that half the members may be from the entourage of the local chief, who in Ghanaian custom is still a man whose leadership is respected and followed, and without whose collaboration community development could be crippled. This leads one to revert, however, to the anomalous relationship which has existed in the past in Ghana between community development and local government, and which was discussed on page 177.

This account of contemporary local government can only sketch the legislative beginnings. At the time of writing there is no experience on which to draw, and it is impossible to know whether this new experiment in local administration will succeed or fail. During the last twenty-five years the elements constituting local government in Ghana have been so varied and cosmopolitan as to defy the sort of classification which Professor Alderfer attempted (p. 17). Before 1951 there was centralized administration on the pattern of France, with native authorities playing a minor and closely supervised rôle. There was then a swing towards the heady freedom of English local government. Then gradually, as Nkrumah's 'democratic centralism' took control, there was an infusion of the forms and vocabulary of Communism. Through all these changes the power of the natural rulers ebbed and flowed, but was never wholly extinguished and has now been partially restored.

So far Ghana has relied a good deal on foreign ideas in local government, and the time must come when it evolves some of its own. The situation we have been describing may be a step nearer to that ideal.

CHAPTER 11

Nigeria

IN order to pick up the historical threads it will be necessary to arrange this chapter in terms of the former Eastern, Western and Northern Regions of Nigeria; though it must be emphasized at the outset that after the three Regions had been superseded by twelve States patterns of local government which had developed certain Regional characteristics became more varied and began to differ from one new State to another. We shall be looking at a number of these new State patterns in due course, though as we said in the Preface to this book the time of writing is an unpropitious one, since in some places administrative order is only beginning to emerge from the chaos of the war, and even in the places less affected by the conflict post-war changes are only beginning to take root. Accordingly, what we can describe are plans rather than achievements.

It is entirely natural, and in accord with the general principles that we discussed in chapter 2, that such variety should increase rather than diminish. It is a platitude that the boundaries of Nigeria, as of all former African colonial dependencies, are artificial and have no basis in sociological fact; this is almost equally true of the old internal Regional boundaries, and the States themselves are a compromise between natural affinity and administrative efficiency. In a country like Nigeria almost any political boundary must be a compromise, and even within most State boundaries there must be minorities, and inequalities in the size of ethnic and linguistic groups. The Western State happens to be predominantly Yoruba and the East Central predominantly Ibo, but States like the Mid-West and the North-East contain great disparities. Local government must reflect such realities, even if State and Federal Government have to compromise with them.

The 1950s and 1960s, however, were a time when the three Regional Governments, especially in the East and West, were seeking uniformity, and we must begin each main section of this chapter by briefly examining the events of those years.[1]

THE EASTERN REGION

The Government of the Eastern Region of Nigeria must take the credit—or accept the responsibility—for being the first West African Government formally to abolish native administration and to replace it by a more forward-looking type of local government. Elsewhere the old Nigerian Native Authority Ordinance, amended at various times, and notably in 1943 and 1948, continued in force for a few more years.

Admittedly the East had more cause to be dissatisfied with its native authorities than the other Regions of Nigeria, for they were based on an enormous number of 'native courts' which themselves had no roots in native custom, and neither the so-called warrant chiefs nor court clerks had the respect of the people, being creatures of the British Administration. The fact was that the structure of society, and notably of Ibo society, did not lend itself to the creation of viable local councils. It was a fragmented society, governed as much by local mass meetings as by chiefs and elders, and the attempt to apply to it the colonial principles of indirect rule had resulted in a huge and unmanageable number of native authorities. At the end of the Second World War efforts were made to reduce them

[1] For a fuller account, valid up to about 1964, see the author's chapter on Local Government in *Nigerian Government and Politics*, John P. Mackintosh, Allen and Unwin, 1965.

in number, but as late as 1948 there were no fewer than 217 native authorities and 300 subordinate native authorities, all very small and mostly quite ineffective. The Eastern House of Assembly addressed itself with great enthusiasm to the task of modernization, and as a result of an immense amount of travel and research on the part of Members and their civil servants they produced the pioneer Local Government Ordinance of 1950.

But although it was a pioneer piece of legislation it was not a successful one. This does not alter the fact that it was a landmark which cannot be removed, and although at a distance of twenty years we can see what was wrong with it, at the time it raised great enthusiasm. It followed the English system far too closely, reproducing all the complexity of three tiers of councils operating independently of each other, the English device of precepting— even the English nomenclature. It gave to these councils far greater powers, including the power of taxation, than had ever been accorded to the native authorities, but simultaneously removed the restraining hand of the District Officer of Government. It was the excellent intention to introduce the Ordinance gradually in selected and carefully prepared places (starting with Ikot Ekpene), but political pressures made this impossible, and it was soon applied, with insufficient preparation, throughout the Region.

It was an act of faith by the Regional Government, but it proved to have been misguided. Councillors soon embarked on the long, sad story of corruption and nepotism which has been the bugbear of local government throughout West Africa, and councillors and staff alike found the system too complicated; they wanted one kind of local council, not three, and the Government was soon faced with demands for 'secession', i.e. for the districts—the middle tier—to be made independent of the upper tier, the 'county'. To its embarrassment, but also to its great credit, the Government decided to deal firmly with irresponsibility, and in the Local Government Law of 1955 restored the direct authority of the Minister, and of the administrative officers of Government, who became in effect a local government 'inspectorate'. The difficulty about the multiplicity of councils dragged on for some time after this, mitigated by various shifts and compromises, but in 1958 the Government bowed to the inevitable, and by administrative action abolished the upper and lower tiers and concentrated on the middle tier—the 'district' as it would normally be called, though in the changing and confusing nomenclature of the time it continued to be called the 'county'.

The hope was that the new counties would be small enough to engage the people's interest but large enough to exercise reasonable powers and duties. In fact, their resources were too small to allow them to be effective except within a very narrow range, consisting mainly of minor roads and small dispensaries. To make matters worse the urge towards secession continued unabated, and by 1960 the number of councils had grown to 107, at which point the Government called a halt in a consolidating Local Government Law of that year, which also introduced full adult franchise in place of the former indirect system of election and—somewhat unexpectedly—gave a fifth of the places on the councils to the recently recognized chiefs and clan heads.

These first ten years of local government, following the Ordinance of 1950, had been a time of constant change and on the whole of failure and disappointment. From the 1960 Law onwards things started to improve, and although progress was uneven some of the better established councils began to show the kind of results that the 1950 Ordinance had envisaged. There was still irresponsibility and mismanagement, but on the other hand surcharges for improper expenditure diminished and there was a general improvement in administration. Nearly half the county councils were budgeting for £50,000 or more, a modest enough figure compared with the need, but enough to test the quality of councillors and staff. A tenth were even graded as efficient by the Government auditors, again a modest figure, but an advance on the universal inefficiency of the first ten years. They were spending something of the order of £4 million, which with the £1 million being spent by the larger urban authorities was a fifth of the total public expenditure for the Region, and their contribution in the field of primary education, health and public works was substantial. The detailed happenings of the early 1960s are perhaps of no great interest today, but it is necessary to emphasize that until the secession of 'Biafra' brought normal administration to a halt local government in Eastern Nigeria, after much failure and discouragement, was beginning to find its feet.

The Eastern States

In the chaos that followed the civil war it might have been expected that local government would have been forgotten and that there would have been a long period of direct central administration. This did not happen, for although what emerged in 1971 was far removed from what had just been coming to fruition before the war, much thought and imagination went into rehabilitating the region through some form of *localized* administration, especially in the South-Eastern and East Central States.

The South-Eastern State

The Military Government of the South-Eastern State at Calabar has resolved on a wholly new departure, which purports to abolish local government altogether. This was a decision arrived at while the war was still in progress and implemented in the latter part of 1970, in a mood of complete disillusionment with what had gone before. The Government would not, it seems, have subscribed to the view we have just advanced, namely that pre-war local government had been making any progress at all.

The philosophy of the Government is set forth in a

Policy Statement[2] couched in terms of great bitterness and disillusion. Native administration under the British administrators and local government under Nigerian politicians were alike dismissed as venal, corrupt and irrelevant to the country's needs. The somewhat intemperate language of this document is balanced by its good sense in identifying certain essentials—that man-power resources were not sufficient to staff both central and local government and that local government must always be a poor relation with little of its own to contribute; and (somewhat more debatably) that the division of the Region into States had brought the central government sufficiently near to the people to dispense with shared central-local responsibility. The document does not use the terms 'deconcentrated' and 'devolved', but it firmly advocates a system of decentralization represented by what it calls 'single administration', in which the dichotomy between deconcentration and devolution is abolished. Local government is dismissed as 'useless duplication'.

It is true that the State Government at Calabar is nearer to the people than the former Regional Government at Enugu, but the South-Eastern State is none the less large and its communications are poor. Accordingly there still needs to be some intermediate link between Government and people, to replace the discredited local government link, if there is to be that 'association' between the two that is a constant theme of the Policy Statement. What was proposed, and what was in fact later implemented in the Development Administration Edict No. 27 of June 1970, was a new form of 'development administration'. We must briefly examine how this differs from 'local government'.

The administrative framework is 140 'Area Development Committees' which include, according to local geography, anything from twenty to forty 'constituent villages', with separate arrangements for the townships, and these form

[2] The Policy of the Military Government of the South-Eastern State on the Abolition of the Local Government System. Government Printer, Calabar, 1968, price 1s 6d.

the base of a shallow pyramid of which the next level is eleven 'Divisional Development Councils'. On the strength of these bare facts an obvious criticism would be that this is simply the old local government with a new label, and it is important to see where the difference lies.

Neither the divisional councils nor the area committees are executive bodies, nor do they have any staff, nor any premises beyond a room in which to meet. The staffs of the old local government councils have been absorbed into the civil service and such assets as the councils possessed transferred to the divisional organization of the central departments. This leaves the 'deconcentrated' divisional organization of Government in full administrative and executive command. The councils and committees are accordingly advisory. Their members will no doubt be elected in the course of time (though for the duration of military rule they will be nominated by the Military Governor) but their chairmen are, and will presumably remain, Government appointees in the manner of the new Ghanaian district council chairmen; moreover, on appointment they become 'public servants'. Councillors are no longer paid anything but their out-of-pocket expenses.

In the process of association between Government and people the area development committees are intended to be the *initiating* bodies, calling attention to local needs and proposing plans and priorities; the divisional councils are *co-ordinating* bodies, reviewing area development plans and forwarding them to Government in the light of their own priorities and recommendations; but *implementation* rests with the divisional agencies of Government, who have the necessary resources.

The differences between old and new are therefore fundamental. Local government has been abolished and a chain of advisory bodies established in its place. On the other hand several important questions remain unanswered. The brief of the committees and councils is 'community development', but the expression is undefined in the Edict in any practical terms, and it is not clear how it differs from the brief of the local government councils, who in spite of their many failings were providing roads, schools, dispensaries and other kinds of 'development' in the broad sense of that word. The policy statement says explicitly that the change of name from 'local government' to 'development' is intended to symbolize the 'desired shift in the social objectives and attitudes of the people', but it does not say what kind of shift it is that is desired. People have always wanted much the same things, and the point at issue is whether one way of trying to satisfy their wants is likely to be more successful than another.

There can be no doubt that local government had completely discredited itself in the former Calabar Province and this new start can only be welcomed. The Government's diagnosis of what was wrong was penetrating; their determination to simplify the new arrangements was sensible; their clarion call to councillors and people to put old corrupt ways behind them and respond to selfless nation-building leadership wholly admirable. Their main practical difficulty may be to keep arrangements simple, i.e. to resist demands for a bigger local organization, bigger premises, bigger allowances; the Edict does in fact provide for the possibility of a local tax or levy for certain purposes, and this would inevitably bring organization in its train. It has also been the universal experience that advisory bodies get tired of being advisory and want to exercise power.

More fundamental criticisms were expressed by the late Alhaji Ali Akilu, who was commissioned by the Governor when the war was over to examine the whole administrative structure of the new State.[3] He thought that the definition of the councils' and committees' rôles was far too academic:

[3] Akilu Commission of Inquiry into the Administrative Structure of the South Eastern State. Report and Recommendations. Ministry of Information and Cultural Affairs, 1970. 5s.

'(*a*) the identification of the areas of economic and social responsibility; and

(*b*) the creation, direction and control of economic and social action in the areas identified for the maximisation of enjoyment by the community of the social product.'

and he drew attention to the paradox inherent in all community development, namely that if it isn't organized nothing happens and that if it *is* organized it ceases to be community development. Specifically, he thought that the appointment of chairmen with the status of public officers was difficult to reconcile with grass-roots participation, which is the essence of community development.

Human nature being what it is, the South-Eastern proposals have already been widely criticized in other parts of Nigeria. Perhaps in three years' time it will be possible to say whether the South-East is going to confound its critics.

The East Central State

Developments in the home State of the Ibo people have a special interest. It may seem surprising that the people most shattered by the civil war should show such resilience that within a year of the war's end they should be making new experiments in local government; in fact, these matters had been under consideration before armed conflict broke out, from the time the Military Government dissolved all local government councils, together with the old Provincial Assemblies, early in 1966. What has emerged after the replacement of the twelve Provinces of the Eastern Region by the three Eastern States has something in common with what emerged in Ghana after the return of civilian government—the replacement of 'local government' by 'local administration', which is a recurring theme of this book. It has, however, an added and unique interest in that the attempt has been made at the village level to harness ancient indigenous patterns of organization and systems of authority—under the generic terms 'communities'—to modern development.

The social organization of the Ibos has always had an important influence on development, and their lineage groups, clans, age-groups and 'town'[4] unions have probably been as effective in bringing progress to the villages as the statutory local authorities. The 'union' organization indeed spread among Ibos living 'abroad', e.g. in Lagos, Kano or even overseas, and resulted in large sums of money being sent back to home villages for improved living, for school scholarships in Nigeria and for higher education bursaries overseas. In some ways this 'tribal' form of organization served its generation better than statutory local government, being spontaneous, enthusiastic and free from the corruption that has always battened on imported forms of administration. In the chaos after the war, and with the dissolution of the former local authorities, it was the salvation of the rural areas. Now for the first time the law gives it recognized status as an agency of community development.

With the abolition of the county councils local administration has reverted to the 'Division', but the 55 divisions of Provincial days have been reduced to 34, with populations of between 100,000 and 300,000; three of them—Enugu, Aba and Onitsha—are 'urban divisions' with specifically urban characteristics. There are divisional councils, but like the regional councils in Ghana, which they resemble in miniature, they have crossed the line which divides 'devolution' from 'deconcentration' and they are in effect an expression of local administration rather than of local government. They are representative in the sense that they include a member from each 'community council' (described below), as well as traditional or chiefly office-holders and co-opted members; but their meetings are attended by the chief departmental officers stationed in the division, and at their head is the Divisional Officer,[5] who appoints their Secretary. The councils' staffs are also mem-

---

[4] Usually meaning a group of villages.

[5] In the three urban divisions he has, somewhat strangely, been given the old title of Resident.

bers of the public service, and the idea of a local government service has lapsed. With regard to councillors, selection or appointment is preferred to election, of which the former Eastern Region had a surfeit before the war.

The divisional councils have taken over the principal functions of the old county councils (minor roads, health services and water supplies) but in the main they are also concerned with the maintenance of law and order, including by-laws, and with co-ordinating the work of the community councils below them. But the old county council services and the new divisional council plans are *implemented* by the Divisional Officer and his government departmental staff.

Although the councils are in a legal sense the 'local authorities' for the divisions, what we have in fact is an acceptance, in miniature, of the prefectorial system of Provincial France or, what amounts to much the same thing, a reversion to the 'DO' system of the colonial era, with Africans in place of expatriates and community councils in place of native authorities.

It is impossible to generalize about the community councils, since it is of their essence that their boundaries follow traditional patterns of 'quarter' and 'kindred', and although these have common elements throughout the State there are also divergencies, for example among the plural communities of the towns or in places where chiefs or traditional office-holders are of more than ordinary significance. Accordingly each community council is created by an *ad hoc* instrument. In general, membership is more flexible than the membership of the former local authorities—for example, public servants living in the neighbourhood (other than 'administrative' officers in the narrow sense) are now encouraged to become members in order to call upon as much local talent as possible; obviously the councils would be strengthened by the addition of local professional or technically qualified residents.

Constitutionally, however, community councils, although indigenous in form and flexible in membership, are none the less part of the Government's local administration, for the Divisional Officer supervises their work and the staff of which he is in charge are now members of the State's civil service, to which—as in the South East—members of the old local government staffs were transferred. Moreover the local representatives of the Ministries of Education, Agriculture and Natural Resources, Works and Transport, Trade and Industry and Social Welfare attend their meetings as *ex officio* members. Accordingly the councils are in part a gathering of all the talents and in part an extension of the central government. They do, on the other hand, elect their own chairman and vice-chairman, unlike the district councils in Ghana or the area development committees in the South-Eastern State.

As to their functions, potentially they can do almost everything that the old local councils could do, save for the county council functions now reserved for the divisional level; but like the former local authorities, what they can do will largely be determined by how much money they can raise, or how much the Government can give them.

THE WESTERN REGION

The Local Government Ordinance of 1950 in the East was followed two years later by the Western Region's Local Government Law of 1952, the Western watershed between native administration and local government. For some years before this the Colonial Government, aware that the Obas and their councils hardly accorded with the Colonial Office's new ideas of efficient and democratic local government, had been trying by every means in their power to modernize the native authorities and to introduce educated young men into councils that were largely elderly and illiterate. The colonial administrators of the time deserve credit for what they were trying to do, for while they realized that the native authorities were inadequate for the 1960s they also believed—and in this they were undoubtedly right—that a foreign system of local government would not rest easily on the social structure of the Yorubas or the people of the Mid-West. They therefore hoped to make the best of both worlds by a policy of gradualism. But the new Action Group Government had little use for gradualism, and quickly introduced a long and complicated enabling law drawing on both British practice and the Eastern Regional Ordinance, with some improvements of their own. It was a considerable feat of legal drafting, which achieved such a high degree of flexibility that both the status and the functions of local authorities could be varied almost without limit to suit particular local circumstances. Essentially, however, it reproduced two features which had caused difficulty in the East (as in Ghana), namely a 'tiered' system (divisional, urban or rural district, and local), and provision for precepting. It did not on the other hand repeat the worst mistake of the Eastern Region in giving the new councils a free hand, but established both a Local Government Inspectorate and a Local Government Service Commission.

However, the pros and cons of this law, or a comparison of its virtues and defects as compared with the laws in the East and in Ghana, are only of academic interest today; for in spite of immensely hard work by politicians and civil servants, and despite some short-term successes, it was in the long run a failure. Its achievements should not be overlooked. By the end of the first ten years (1952–62) recurrent expenditure by local authorities had risen from £1·9 million to £8·4 million, over 30% of this sum being spent on education and 12% on health services; capital expenditure was certainly low, but in 1962 half a million pounds was spent by local authorities on minor roads and bridges, maternity centres and dispensaries, markets and motor parks.

But whereas in the East, after the first ten years of comparative failure, some at least of the county councils were beginning to find their feet, in the West the various divisional, district and local councils went from bad to worse. As early as 1958 the Government had had to introduce a Local Government Amendment Law which enabled the Governor to appoint either a 'sole administrator' or a 'committee of management' to perform the duties of a council which had become intolerably corrupt or inefficient; and by 1965 every one of them had been suspended. It was difficult at times to separate corruption from a senseless kind of party politics, for sometimes it appeared that councils were suspended for corruption when their offence was political. Be that as it may, the councils had to be suspended either because their corruption was blatant or because they had degenerated into quarrelling political factions.

To make matters worse the experience of the East (and later of Ghana) was repeated in that the public generally could not envisage anything so large as the upper tier (in this case the division) as the unit for representative government, and agitated for something smaller. Politicians gave way to constituency pressures for fragmentation, and although no amending legislation was ever passed the flexible provisions of the law were used to let divisional councils lapse in one place after another. Meanwhile the 'local' councils were proving too small to be useful, and since they depended entirely on the Government to keep them going the Government simply let them die. The result was a tendency for the unit of local government to become the rather unsatisfactory middle-sized unit—the district—which was not big enough in resources to do anything very effective and not small enough to mean very much to the man in the bush. Some divisional—and indeed some local—councils continued, and so flexible was the Law that all three survive at the time of writing in both West and Mid-West States. But in general the drift was towards a middle-sized district whose resources were too small for effectiveness.

A succession of political crises, interspersed with eight months of emergency administration by the Federal Government, made the task of administering the Western Region in the early 1960s almost impossible. This was particularly tragic, because paradoxically the central civil service was rich in imagination, and more serious thought was given to the fundamental principles of local government and their most fruitful application in local circumstances than anywhere else in West Africa. There had been much painstaking research, for example, into the important question of what was the optimum size of population, area and revenue to support schools (in terms of inspectors), medical and health services (in terms of beds, doctors and nurses), or public works (in terms of machinery, staff and equipment). These are fundamental matters which had never before been considered objectively, or translated into terms of efficient administration. The provisional conclusion that the Ministry of Local Government had reached was that each of these major services needed a different radius within which to work, and that therefore there ought to be individual 'Service Authorities', differing from each other but of a size much greater than the district councils; but that in order that they should not become mere field units of government departments they should be controlled by bodies indirectly elected from the district and the surviving local councils. This would have needed a radical reform of the law, but in the meantime a partial approach towards it had been made by taking advantage of a section of the 1952 Law which allowed the setting up of Joint Boards of local authorities for 'the joint operation of any work or service'. By the time of the 1966 crisis there were some thirty such Boards, dealing with forestry, water supplies, police and education.

But talent and ideas were allowed to run to waste, and at the end of the civil war local government in the West and Mid-West was basically as it had been created by the 1952 Law, as amended and consolidated in 1957.

The Western State

Although disappointments in the West were similar to those experienced in Calabar, the Western Government has taken a very different course from that of the South-Eastern

State. Instead of abolishing local government it has taken the institution as it survived the war and has concentrated on improving it at what experience had shown to be its two weakest points, namely the inferior status, and hence quality, of its staff, which inhibited recruitment and lowered efficiency; and the multiplicity of small councils with which the previous civilian administration had been so deeply concerned.

The Ministry of Local Government *Circular No. 1*, dated January 1971, took an important step forward by putting local government staff on a basis of full equality with the civil service; that is to say a local government officer and a civil servant with the same qualifications would have the same pay and status. This is hardly a definitive solution to a very thorny problem, because whatever may be said about 'parity of esteem' ambitious young men will probably think that the civil service has the advantage both in prestige and prospects. On the other hand it will at least help to bridge the gap between the two, and with the rising cost of living in the capital city some may come to realize that in a smaller place the same pay really means more pay, and that there is much to be said, to use an English metaphor, for being a big fish in a small pond rather than a small fish in a big pond.

As to larger units, there is, as we have seen, nothing new about the proposal. The difference is that the pre-war Government could never move in the matter because of political warfare, whereas with the suspension of party politics the Military Government can achieve by Edict what their predecessors failed to achieve by reason and persuasion.

As we have already said, all elected councillors had been suspended by 1965, and for some years administrators or appointed committees ran the authorities with the help of their staffs. In 1969, however, they were supplemented by 'advisory committees' comprising ten unpaid members, with District Officers of Government as chairmen. This move, however tentative, towards a return to local representation was hastened by the dissatisfaction and rioting in 1968 against the imposition of taxes—the cry of 'no taxation without representation' being a universal one.[6]

At the time of writing 114 councils survive under the 1957 Law, but the Government has announced its intention of reducing them to 51. There is very great variety in the size and financial viability of the existing councils. One divisional council (Ife) budgets for over £250,000 and ten others between £100,000 and £200,000. On the other hand a score spend less than £10,000, while there is a large block in the middle between £25,000 and £50,000. The proportions spent on pure administration are equally varied— a quarter, a third, in two cases over a half; but save in the half dozen largest technical staff are painfully few. Typically there may be a few dispensers and health inspectors, but plumbers, electricians and other qualified artisans —to say nothing of qualified works foremen—are few and far between. The hope is that the higher pay and status promised under circular 1/71, and the larger size of the authorities, will help to attract them.

Presumably by the time this book is published the reorganization will have taken place. The Government's White Paper on the subject[7] argues that it is 'fruitless and demoralizing' to maintain the existing small and ineffective units and sets out the various criteria by which a workable compromise has to be made. It is intended that the day-to-day administration of the fifty-one new 'local government administrations' shall be the responsibility of chief executive officers with wide powers, and as a corollary of this the over-sophisticated committee system, which fragments the work of councils and hampers a chief executive officer's

[6] There was also a reduction in the amount of the tax, accompanied by an effort on the part of the Government to release arrears of money owing to the councils in the form of PAYE refunds on incomes up to £300, which is theirs by right but which as a matter of convenience and economy the Government collects.

[7] Proposals for the Reorganization of Local Government Councils. Western State Official Document No. 4 of 1971. Government Printer, Ibadan.

work, will be abolished. Instead there is to be one Standing Committee which will consider policy and prepare the Council's business.

It seems to be agreed that although these fifty-one authorities ought to be no smaller if they are to be efficient they are still too large to give most people a sense of participation or the feeling that they are being *represented*. Accordingly small towns, villages and other district communities will continue to be identified, and will be represented by an 'Area Committee'. These committees could hardly be called a 'second tier' of local government, since like the area development committees in the South-East their function will only be to discuss, initiate and make proposals to the council of the local government administration, but they will not have the resources to carry them out; an interesting proposal, however, is that if a council is unable to support an area committee's proposals they must nevertheless be forwarded to the Ministry for their consideration. Forty per cent of the money raised within an area must be spent within that area; it has always been a matter of controversy that taxes gathered in one part of a Division, a State, or even within the whole Federation of Nigeria should be spent for the benefit of another part, and the 40% formula represents a compromise between the two criteria of 'derivation' and 'need'.

The place of chiefs is regarded differently from that in Ghana, where their participation in local government has been restored (p. 173). In the Western State the principle is that there are to be insulated from the work of local government administrations (except that they may continue to act as ceremonial Presidents where that has been the custom); they may however be members of area committees.

At the end of twenty years, therefore, local government in the new State is both simpler and more viable than it was in the old Region. On the other hand it is important to conclude by pointing out that the range of its functions has contracted. This is clearly seen from the fact that the need for the old Joint Boards of local authorities (p. 63) has disappeared; of the functions for which they were responsible local government police are no more, water supplies have become a responsibility of the State (or in the case of major schemes the Federal Government), education has reverted to the *ad hoc* principle and is administered by Local School Boards, and forestry has been nationalized. It should, however, now be possible for the new local authorities to do a more realistic job, even if they operate within a smaller compass.

In contrast to the Eastern States, local government staff keep their own identity, under a Local Government Service Board, and have not become civil servants; they have, however, as we have seen, been placed on a basis of equality with them.

The Mid-West State

For ten years the Mid-West and Western States were one, and it is only natural that strong resemblances should survive in their local government organization. There are still more similarities than differences, and there is not a great deal to add to what has been said about the Western State.

Equality between central and local government service has been accepted in principle in Benin as well as in Ibadan, though a Circular 1/71 has yet to appear. The rationalization of council areas is moving on similar lines —for example district councils in Ishan Division were reduced from eight to three as long ago as 1968, and there is continuous review since then. The so-called 'grading' of councils has ceased, as the policy is to establish *all* councils at a viable level.

Two points of difference are worth noting. Advisory Committees, which previously followed the example of the West, were replaced in January 1971 by 'committees of management'—sometimes divisional, sometimes district, sometimes local; they number between ten and twenty members, but in the light of experience their powers of management are to exclude staff matters and the award of contracts. Second, the Mid-West has always led the way in property rating, which is now established in Benin, Warri, Sapele, Ughelli and Agbor.

THE NORTHERN REGION

In writing of the southern States of Nigeria we briefly sketched the history of local government in the 1950s and 1960s in what used to be the Eastern and Western Regions. Before discussing local administration in the northern States it will be necessary to write rather more fully of the former Northern Region, since its system was profoundly different, and some knowledge of the recent past is necessary for an understanding of the present.

First we must clear away a misconception about 'the North'. People still tend to equate local government in the North with 'powerful emirates', but this is an over-simplification, and two things need to be borne in mind. First that although there are indeed strong and well-organized emirates these were never in themselves the units of local government; these were the 'native authorities', a term which the previous Northern Government chose to retain until 1968 in preference to the more usual 'local' authorities, which it then adopted; it is true that the emirates were co-terminous with the native authorities, that is to say no emirate was split up into more than one native authority, but the two expressions were not strictly speaking inter-changeable; while in areas that were not wholly Muslim a number of 'chieftaincies' joined with others to form 'federated native authorities'. Second, that over substantial parts of the North there are no emirates, since the Hausa-Fulani influence did not fully establish itself over such peoples as the Tiv, Nupe, Igala, Idoma or the Yorubas of Kabba, still less among the many so-called 'pagan' people of the Plateau. It is true that British administration tried to impose a uniform pattern of administration throughout the Region, and to introduce the pattern of emirate rule universally, but experience and growing knowledge of the people led them to modify this policy, and local government in such areas has long been 'conciliar', and sometimes fragmentary. There are in fact astonishing extremes in this country, from strong, disciplined and wealthy emirates of the 'north of the North' to the rudimentary councils of primitive tribes in the hills and plateaux of the south-east.

This brings us to the first of two *fundamental* differences in the recent development of local government. Southern Nigeria and Ghana, faced with the task of modernizing and revitalizing their native authorities, introduced laws which, though more flexible than the British legislation on which they were modelled, were expected to apply more or less uniformly throughout the respective countries; it is true that they were supposed to start experimentally in one or two places first and then to develop in the light of experience, but political pressures soon caused them to be applied wholesale instead of piecemeal, and within a short time of their enactment the terms of these laws were being implemented everywhere. The Northern Government set its face against this, and while accepting the principle that the NAs must become more representative and more efficient, to keep pace with modern development, they resolved that this principle should be applied to each NA in the light of its history, its existing circumstances and its potentialities. To impose the same pattern of local government in Sokoto and on the Mambila Plateau would have been manifestly absurd. Accordingly, instead of providing for 'tiers' of councils with specific names, the Native Authority Law of 1954 made a much more flexible arrangement, under which the Premier could constitute as a native authority 'any chief or person, any chief or person in council or any chief or person *and* council', while the Minister of Local Government could similarly constitute 'any council or any group of persons'. The intention behind this was flexibility, which would start with the situation as it actually was, but would allow for change and progress;

as we shall see in a moment, this intention has been fulfilled.

The second fundamental difference, though this applied more strongly in the emirates than elsewhere, was that native administration had long occupied a place of importance in the administration of the country comparable to that of local government in Britain. While the southern Nigerian and Ghanaian councils were gradually working up to a larger share in the administration of the country, though leaning heavily on government departmental assistance, the NAs virtually *were* the administration of the country. The larger ones carried, as in the successor States they still carry, responsibility for the major social services. For example, according to the latest figures available[8] the Kano Local Authority has a revenue of £2·9 million, Bornu and Sokoto £1·5 million, and Katsina £1·2 million. These are figures of a totally different order from the local authorities in the south of Nigeria or in Ghana or Sierra Leone. Even in the middle ranges there are authorities like the Tiv (£657,000) and Ilorin (£529,000); indeed the smallest in the North tends to correspond to the average in the South. It used to be said with some truth that before the reorganization into States that if the central government collapsed the NAs would carry on the administration of the country, whereas if the NAs collapsed there would be complete disaster!

The starting point for reorganization under the régime of the new States was therefore entirely different from elsewhere in West Africa.

The Native Authority Law of 1954

We have mentioned the laws[9] of 1950, 1951 and 1952 in Eastern Nigeria, Ghana and Western Nigeria respectively as the watersheds between the old native administration

[8] Northern States of Nigeria Local Government Year Book 1970.

[9] It is difficult to be accurate about nomenclature, as legislation during the 1950s was at different times and places described in terms of Ordinances, Acts or Laws.

and the new local government. The corresponding law in Northern Nigeria, in so far as it can be equated with them, was passed in 1954, but it was more of a consolidating measure and less of a new departure. It permitted a remarkable degree of flexibility in the composition of the authorities as between the respective influences of the chiefs and of traditional, nominated and elected members, and allowed for a gradual widening of their representative character. For example, when the Law was passed three-quarters of the NA councils had a majority membership comprising chiefs and either traditional or nominated members, but within ten years more than half had an elected majority.

Councillors and Staff in the NA System

We now come to some important departures from what was written in previous chapters about the work of the councillors and the position of the staff. In southern Nigeria and Ghana the intention was to emulate the British practice whereby councillors take no part in administration, and when, as often happened, they started giving directions to the staff or taking part in the ordinary work of the office, it was regarded as wrongful interference. In Northern Nigeria, however, councillors have long been associated with administration, partly because this was inherent in the traditional system handed down from long ago, and partly because in many areas of the North there were too few educated men in the 1950s to form local bureaucracies, or at any rate to provide the kind of senior local government officials who could take the initiative, make decisions and implement policy. Accordingly, NA councils bore some resemblance to miniature 'cabinets', in which selected councillors held portfolios and were put in charge of the various departments of the NAs work in return for a full-time salary. There would be a Member in charge of public health, education, works, agriculture, forestry and so on, and his responsibility, in the limited sphere of the NA, would be comparable to that of a Minister in the wider sphere of the Region. With the rapid increase of education, and more particularly of local government training, the quality of the staff of the NAs is showing consistent improvement, and as this happens the amount of detailed work by the 'executive councillors' may diminish. Nevertheless the principle is still followed that certain councillors are responsible for certain branches of work, and this is a radical difference from the system we have been discussing hitherto, where responsibility is vested in committees. There can be little doubt that as the committee system develops in the North, and especially in the emirates, the authority of the executive councillor will diminish further in proportion; by Ministerial direction, there were at least two committees set up by every NA, a finance committee and an establishment (or appointments) and staff committee.

Meanwhile, because of the great size of some of the NAs (the Bornu NA was larger than the former Eastern Region of Nigeria) a standing Executive Committee is frequently appointed, instead of the various 'functional' committees of British practice. Indeed, the words 'cabinet' and 'parliamentary' have sometimes been used to distinguish between the very large NAs of the north of the Region and the smaller ones of the south and east, where an orthodox committee system is more practicable. Though neither adjective is very accurate they draw attention to a real difference, but one that is likely to diminish rather than grow.

District Heads and the 'Chain of Command'

An even more fundamental difference between the North of Nigeria and the rest of West Africa lies in the hierarchy of 'local government officials' right down to the smallest village or quarter of a town. The word 'official' is really not an appropriate one, since many of the posts of district and village heads are hereditary, or restricted to certain families, and they are often given the general description of 'traditional heads'; they are in fact persons of considerable status in their own right, and could hardly be described as employees. They are appointed by the emir or chief, subject to the approval of Government, and they represent something that does not exist in southern Nigeria, that is a chain of authority reaching down directly from the NA to the smallest community within its borders. It is because of them that the mechanics of a large operation, like a census, an election or the annual tax collection, work more smoothly in Northern Nigeria than elsewhere; indeed the equivalent of an annual census is taken for the assessment of tax, which is one of the major responsibilities of the district head, and a very high proportion of the tax—estimated at well over 90%—is collected each year without difficulty.

It is sometimes thought that this chain of command, as we have called it, is in itself undemocratic, especially as the offices of heads are traditional, and derive from an ancient and authoritarian system. We are confronted with two points of view; twentieth-century bureaucratic procedures demand that every holder of a public office should appear on a short list and be interviewed by a committee; in Northern Nigeria a traditional office is being adapted to an increasingly representative form of local government; and there is no question that the *work* of a district head is thoroughly modern.

Be this as it may, the system is one of the most important departures from what was described in the earlier chapters of this book; it applies particularly to the emirates, since district heads do not exist, or exist in a modified form, in the conciliar native authorities of the south and east of the Region. Village headmen, on the other hand, are universal throughout the North; they were the foundation on which native administration was built and are equally vital to the local government of today.

The Revenue of Northern Local Authorities

In Chapter 7 we discussed the revenue of local authorities in general terms—i.e. in terms which could be applied to local government in many parts of the world. The methods of revenue raising that were described are employed in varying degrees in Sierra Leone, Ghana and southern Nigeria, but we have not described in detail how they are currently applied in those countries because practice changes so frequently that it would be impossible to do so with any hope of accuracy. A word must be said, however, about the sources of revenue of local authorities in the North of Nigeria, since they differ from the norm, and Chapter 7 did not mention them.

They are first the Community Tax (*Haraji*) and second the Cattle Tax (*Jangali*). We noted that in the Western State the Government collected income tax through the PAYE procedure and remitted to the local authorities all tax on income of £300 a year and less. In the Northern States it is the other way round, for except in Kwara State the local authorities act as collectors for Government both of personal tax directly assessed by the State Revenue Division, and of PAYE deductions from the salaries of local government employees. This personal tax is now known as the 'community tax', and under the Personal Tax Law 1962 $87\frac{1}{2}\%$ was retained by the native authorities. This percentage now stands at 80, except in the North Western State where at the time of writing it is 75.

The importance of cattle tax naturally varies from one part of the Northern States to another, but *haraji* and *jangali* between them account for about 65% of the total revenue of local authorities; Government grants amount to 20% and the rest comes from various local sources.

We have now summarized the principal differences between the northern and the southern States of Nigeria, and it is now time to look more closely at the contemporary picture in the six northern States.

The Northern States

Each State, shortly after its creation, appointed a committee to study and make recommendations on the reform of local government. White Papers or similar public documents were published on what they had to say, and this was followed by legislation (by Edict) at various times between the end of 1968 and the beginning of 1970. The result, as was to be expected, is that local government has fallen into six different patterns. Some of them bear strong resemblances to each other, though no two are exactly alike; on the other hand differences between the Hausa-Fulani emirates and the disparate peoples further south naturally remain. Since there *are* certain similarities and common patterns, however, it would be unprofitable to describe developments State by State, and it will be best to take some principle themes and to illustrate variations on these themes from the various States.

What's in a name?

Before doing so it would be appropriate to salute the end of the old and honourable expression 'Native Authority'. It was not, of course, so regarded in other parts of West Africa, where the pejorative word 'native' was abolished many years ago in place of the more acceptable 'local'. The difficulty about taking this step in the North was that the form of local government known as the 'NA' had become an accepted part of life and had even passed—as E'Ne'—into the Hausa language. Since to most people it was just a familiar word describing the only sort of government they really understood the former Regional Government clung to it with surprising tenacity long after it had passed into disuse elsewhere. However, it was impossible that such a dubious word as 'Native' should survive indefinitely, however much goodwill surrounded it, and the new State Governments quickly abolished it.

Unfortunately they did not agree on a single common phrase to succeed it, and in what seems to be an unnecessary piece of confusion its successor is variously called a local authority, a local government authority and a local administration. The fine shades of the English language in this field, with their acquired as well as their original meanings, have always been a cause of difficulty.

Structural changes

Turning to more substantial matters, there have been organizational changes affecting State, Province and Division. In four States separate Ministries of Local Government have been established, and departments responsible for Community Development have been merged with them. This is a point of some significance, for it suggests that in this part of West Africa at least the view is taken that local government and community development are indissoluble. A Policy Statement from Benue-Plateau State is even more specific:

> '. . . a new Ministry for Local Government and Social Development has been created as a result of which there have now been brought under one umbrella Local Government, Community Development, Social Welfare and Home Economics, thus emphasizing the close relationship which these units have with one another.'

In the Kano and North-Eastern States, on the other hand, local government is supervised by a special Division of the Military Governor's Office.

A more significant change is that in four States the old Provincial organization has been abolished on the ground that the substitution of State for Region has rendered it superfluous. Government, it was argued, now needed only one intermediate link with the people, and this would be provided by local government; indeed, it was thought that the Province was positively holding back progress by blocking the channels of communication between central and local government. But in the other two States, North-Eastern and North-Central, it has been retained for the very reason that it eases communication. The retention of Provinces tends to correlate with the abolition of Divisions, and *vice versa*. For example Kwara, a relatively fragmented State in former native authority terms, retains eleven divisions in place of the previous seven, and makes the division the keystone of local administration; whereas North-East and North-Central, which have retained the

Provinces which lie within their borders, have done away with divisions. These decisions have turned on the local 'ecology'—size, communications, to some extent ethnic grouping.

Patterns of Local Administration

When we come to look at what has taken the place of the old native authorities the picture is complicated. In some States former NAs have been divided, in others they have been merged, in some there have been both divisions and mergers. There is no great profit in pursuing this particular analysis. Of greater significance is the fact that the six States now fall into three pairs for what might be called their basic local government arrangements.

The first pair, as might be expected, are the two riverine States of *Benue-Plateau and Kwara*, which differ in detail but which basically continue a relatively familiar form of divisional administration. In the former there are nine divisions of which six are co-terminous with newly established 'local administrations' and three are sub-divided, giving a total of fourteen local administrations in all; in the latter, eleven divisions, each co-terminous with a 'local government authority'. There are instances in each State, though there is no uniform pattern, of subordinate local authorities; for example, there are now three subordinate authorities within the former single Tiv Authority.

An important difference between the two States at the time of writing is that the local authorities in Benue-Plateau are governed by appointed councils, whereas in Kwara each division, and hence each new local authority area, is in charge of a Government administrative officer as sole administrator.

The second pair, about which it will be necessary to say rather more since a new administrative concept has been introduced, are *Kano and North-Central*. These States include three of the big classic 'Emirate-NAs'—Kano itself, Katsina and Zaria, as well as a number of small ones—and it is here principally that reforming minds have been at work, for under the new dispensation the Emirate is not quite the monolithic organization of former days.

Two ideas dominate contemporary thinking in the northern States generally—first, to 'bring Government nearer to the people', and second, to promote 'development'. The vehicle by which these two objects are to be achieved in Kano and North-Central is a new piece of administrative machinery known as an Administrative Area. The size of an area can be roughly judged from the fact that there are four in the Kano Emirate (excluding Kano Metropolitan) and ten in the North Central State; by and large an area includes the territories of not less than three and not more than seven district heads. An area is presided over by an administrative officer, with a council (at present nominated but potentially to be elected) on which the district heads sit *ex officio*. It is expected to be the initiating body for 'development' and has attached to it a full range of departmental officers. It retains a percentage of the community tax (85% and 80% respectively) and further *ad hoc* grants have been made for initial expenditure, to 'prime the pump'. It is therefore a new tier in the local government structure. Although areas have not yet had a chance to prove themselves, what appear to be the pros and cons?

Their primary purpose is said to be 'to bring local government nearer to the people'. Only experience can show whether administration at the level of half-a-dozen districts is realistically 'nearer', and whether field staffs will be too thinly spread to be effective. There is a danger that they might fall into the same trap as the medium-sized authorities of Ghana and southern Nigeria, of being neither one thing nor the other.

But although it may take some time to prove their value in terms of development, their result in terms of social change is likely to be stimulating, since they will be the point at which two bureaucracies—those of the Emir and of the Commissioner (i.e. Minister) for Local Government—will meet. Generally speaking the two have their own distinctive flavour—a local aristocracy on the one hand and a professional civil service, selected on the strength of education and training, on the other. What is clear is that the district head's allegiance to his Emir, though still paramount, is no longer undivided, for there is a District Officer of Government in charge of the area, whose council meetings the district head attends. As for the Emir, a new tier of local administration is created which is independent, in its allotted sphere, of the Local Authority Council over which he now presides. It is a further adjustment that the Emirs are having to make to what, in the North of Nigeria, is widely called 'modernity'.

It would seem that this intrusion of a piece of Ministry machinery into the organization of an emirate must tend to diminish the authority of the Emir, and there are many who think that this was its deliberate purpose. Others, on the other hand, believe that the natural authority of the emirs among their peoples is so deep-rooted that such administrative changes will do little to diminish it.

Much will depend on how actual functions are divided between State, local authority and area, and this is not finally decided. Judging from what has been decided, the tendency may be to regard the areas as being responsible for 'development from below', meaning minor roads and water supplies, markets and small revenue-earning projects. But equal emphasis is being attached, at the time of writing, to the possible take-over by State Governments of former local authority functions. The old NAs were often notoriously inefficient—because they were not particularly interested—in agriculture, veterinary services and forestry, and the standard of some of their public works, including important roads, was failing to keep up with the times. But if they are to part with functions to the area beneath and to the State above the Emirs who preside over them will find themselves presiding over a diminishing sector.

The third pair are *North-Western* (i.e. Sokoto and three smaller emirates) and *North-Eastern* (Bornu and four smaller authorities).

In these two States the old NAs have simply changed their names to Local Authorities, except that in the North-East some rather unsatisfactory 'federated native authorities' have been unified into a single new local authority. None the less an important change has been introduced in that the new local authorities have been divided into 'Development Areas', to a total of thirty-one in the North-East and twenty-three in the North-West. These are not a new tier of local government, as are the 'administrative' areas of Kano and North-Central, but adjuncts of the local authorities themselves. Their function is to stimulate development within these local authority areas, operating through 'Development Boards' whose executive functions are vested in secretaries from the public service. They bear some resemblance to the community councils of the East-Central State (p. 189) in that they consist partly of local representatives (of the subordinate districts of the local authority) and partly of Government officers concerned with development who are stationed in the area, together with their local authority colleagues. The boards are in fact a congregation of all the best talents available in the vicinity, and their purpose is to develop water supplies, dispensaries, markets and minor roads on the one hand and any commercial activity that the local authorities may delegate to them on the other.

Under these arrangements the emirs and chiefs remain as presidents or chairmen of their local authority councils, and although they now only have casting votes, instead of being 'chiefs-in-council' with formidable personal power, their authority is not further diminished (as it is in Kano and North-Central) by a lower tier under the supervision of a Government administrative officer assuming some of their former responsibilities. District heads, on the other hand, lose the inherent or traditional privileges that many of them have inherited, and become normal members of the public service, in open competition with their colleagues.

The development boards' revenues are derived from an

adjustable percentage of the community tax, Government grants for any specific projects that the Government officers on the boards may recommend, and special rates collected for them by the parent local authority.

Subordinate Local Authorities

The Native Authority Law of 1954 included a radical departure from the local government laws of southern Nigeria and Ghana in that it provided for the establishment of *subordinate* authorities, though this was perhaps not so much a departure as the continuance of a practice which used to be common to all these countries before 1950, but which was discontinued elsewhere. British legislation on local government does not envisage the idea of subordinate authorities, and since southern Nigeria and Ghana followed British legislation they adopted the system of 'tiers' which we have discussed elsewhere.

The subordinate authorities of the NA Law, which survive in the new States, take various forms. In the first place the Law (sections 20–24) allowed for the establishment of subordinate authorities in the full sense, and where this was done the subordinate authority must 'obey the orders of the native authority to which the Governor has directed that it shall be subordinate', but it may also exercise powers delegated to it by the superior authority. We mentioned this practice in describing divisional administration in the Benue-Plateau and Kwara States, instancing the division of the former Tiv Authority into three. But it is common practice throughout the North, there being sixteen subordinate authorities altogether in Benue-Plateau, eight in Kwara, four in North-Central, fifteen in North-East and five in one particular authority in the former Niger Province of the North-West.

The Law also allowed, in section 54, the creation of administrative sub-areas within any native authority, and from a comparative point of view these are of greater interest. The section said that a native authority may 'divide the area under its jurisdiction . . . into districts, village areas, wards and such other administrative sub-areas as it may consider expedient' and goes on to say, in effect, that it may appoint district, village and ward heads. This is the statutory basis of the 'chain of command' which we described on page 202, and which is still the distinguishing mark of the Northern States of Nigeria compared with other parts of West Africa.

The changing position of the 'Chiefs'

In no part of West Africa does the statutory word 'chief' mean so many different things. The Emir of Kano presides over the lives of 794,000 *taxpayers*, the Emir of Wase in the old Plateau Province over 9,000; the Tor Tiv over 198,000, the Olu Bunu in Kwara State over 2,000. Fifteen years ago many chiefs, and in particular of course the great Emirs, wielded more personal power than the paramount chiefs of Ghana or the Obas of Western Nigeria, but this has greatly changed. It is instructive, for example, to observe what happened between 1958 and 1968.

The North has always distinguished between a 'Chief-*in*-Council', meaning a chief who governs but takes advice, and a 'Chief-*and*-Council', meaning one who presides over a more or less representative body. But these terms are imprecise and it is better to look at the exact categories prevailing in the NAs in 1958. They were:

	Native authorities
Chief and traditional members	2
Chief, traditional and nominated members	23
Chief, traditional and nominated members, with elected minority	12
Chief, traditional and nominated members, with 50% elected	3
Chief, traditional and nominated members, with elected majority	23
Wholly elected	1

It is difficult to give an exactly comparable figure for 1968, or for the present day, because elections are suspended until the return of civilian government, and where an elected majority, or a fully elected council, is accepted in principle it is in practice nominated by the State Governor. It is safe to say, however, that the first two categories in the above list have disappeared altogether, that about fifteen councils are in principle wholly elected, and that in the rest Governors have declared that with the return of civilian government there will be an elected majority (generally of two-thirds). The future rôle of the emir or other chief is envisaged as being president or chairman with a casting vote.

The 'Portfolio' Councillors

One of the unresolved problems in most of the Northern States is the future of the executive councillor, who was described on page 201. In the southern States of Benue-Plateau and Kwara, where the office was thought to induce rivalry and ill-feeling, it has been abolished. A more cogent criticism, and one which those States which retain the system will have to consider, could have been that it is difficult to reconcile with another aspect of local government which has caught the favourable attention of West Africans—namely the managerial or 'chief executive officer' system. The portfolio system had much to commend it in the large NAs in the past, especially when the educational standards of the staff were poor. Indeed it can stand on its own merits as a system anywhere; something like it can be discerned in certain kinds of American municipal administration and it has had its open advocates in the United Kingdom. On the other hand it goes against the tide of current opinion and practice elsewhere in West Africa, and the stated policy of the former Northern Regional Government was that it should be 'phased out'.

Local Government Staff

The status of local government staff is another question to which no uniform answer has been found.

In the former Northern Region there was no Local Government Service Board or Commission, as there was in the south, and staffs were responsible only to their immediate employers, the native authorities. On the other hand the Minister of Local Government—and indeed the Premier personally—used to pay close attention to their terms and conditions of service. Establishment Committees were set up in most NAs at the Premier's direction, and he reserved the right to approve salary scales and certain senior appointments, especially in the emirates.

Changing attitudes towards the old NA concepts have caused the question of a 'unified' local government service to be examined for the first time, except in the North-Central State which has decided to continue with the inherited system. The other five States have accepted varying measures of State-wide control, but a study in detail shows how many fine shades of difference this subject can contain. At one end of a spectrum, so to speak, is full integration with the civil service; short of this there is the method (recommended in the North-Eastern State) of occasional inter-change or secondment between the two; again, there may be interchangeability between different local authorities; finally the local authority may continue as the effective employer, but with a Local Government Service Board ensuring comparable conditions of service throughout the State.

Conclusion

This rapid survey of the North has been both selective and superficial, and by the time the book appears it may well contain inaccuracies; for few things are more certain than that patterns of administration will continue to change and details of practice to alter. The survey is justified, however, because it illustrates the argument of the opening chapters of the book—that local government is infinitely adaptable and obeys no universal rules. What is happening in the six States simply illustrates the continuing search for the right answers, and—unfortunately for those who write books—the answers in five years' time will again be different.

At the moment the northern States face a two-fold

challenge in local government, The first is that they have more to live up to than their Nigerian or Ghanaian neighbours, since local government under its old name was always the main instrument of the Administration. The latest available estimates show total recurrent local authority expenditure of over £17½ million, the largest being £4·4 million for the North-East and the smallest £1·3 million for Kwara. These are figures of a different order from those of the southern States; and the North-East's budget is almost as much as that for the whole of local government in Ghana.

The second is that they have to face this challenge under the handicap which the division of the Region into States has brought about. Not only is there the difficult adjustment to a new organization; there is also increased competition for staff. Six civil services instead of one are inevitably attracting young men away from local government into the State ministries or public corporations, and the greatest of all problems in implementing the plans we have described is likely to come from the drift of talent to the six State capitals.

CHAPTER 12

Conclusion

The Swing of the Pendulum
DURING the twenty years 1950–1970 the pendulum first swung from native administration to local government; it has now completed its back-swing, not of course to the point from which it started, because each swing of a pendulum falls short of the previous one, until it reaches equilibrium. However, it has swung back to a point which might be described as *local administration*, an advance in terms of responsible government on the old NAs, but falling far short of what was envisaged in the 1950s. It will probably swing a few more times before it comes to rest, but our task in this concluding chapter is to examine the first swing and counter-swing, and to assess current tendencies and probable future trends.

Except in parts of Northern Nigeria, native administration was a kind of nursery for local government. The expatriate DO—'father to his people'—was fair but strict. He sought advice but he retained control. There was not a great deal that NA councillors could decide for themselves, for any major decision required the DO's approval. Indeed, he was himself a man under authority, and such matters as annual estimates needed the approval of his own superiors in the Resident's or Provincial Commissioner's office. Young educated men were almost entirely absent from the NA councils, whose members were chosen by traditional methods or were nominated. The public at large were more interested in them as courts than as administrative bodies. It had been a useful system in its day, but the ideas liberated by the Second World War had made it obsolete.

The Local Government Laws of 1950 in Eastern Nigeria, 1951 in Ghana and 1952 in Western Nigeria swung immediately to the other extreme. A large majority of councillors was elected by popular franchise (occasionally by indirect election) and the authority of the DO was either abolished, as in Eastern Nigeria, or modified to an advisory rôle.[1] This swing can only be properly understood in a political context. In the early 1950s political independence was in the air (although few people expected it to come as quickly as it did) and so-called political parties, lining up against each other in earnest, saw in the elected councils instruments for their own purposes; in Ghana and Western Nigeria the dominant parties also saw them as weapons with which to diminish the power of the chiefs and their followers; in neither country were the parties opposed to the 'natural rulers' as such, being deeply sensitive to tradition, but they thought with some justification that the colonial power had made use of the chiefs for their own purposes, and had distorted tradition. We use the expression 'so-called' in relation to the political parties because they had no distinctive policies or political beliefs (beyond outbidding each other in their demands for independence), but were in effect rival factions jockeying for the national power that was awaiting whomsoever was in the strongest position when independence came. These considerations were to have a profound effect on local government.

Until this time West African politics had been an affair of the intelligentsia, often members of the aristocratic families. The focal point of their politics was the demand for representation in Government and ultimate national independence, on which they conducted a polite dialogue with an unresponsive British Government. This was swept aside after the Second World War by the advent of the mass political party, which was prepared to get its way by rougher methods. An inevitable consequence was that large numbers of self-seekers—including not a few rogues—

[1] An early development in the Western Region of Nigeria was that DOs came to be called LGAS—'Local Government Advisers'.

found their way into the parties in the wake of respected national leaders, and in particular took a firm grip on the new local government councils. The new system was one which depended heavily on the personal qualities of its elected councillors, since it gave them undeniable power. If they were people of integrity and ability it could work; otherwise it could prove disastrous.

Africans with these qualities from the business and professional classes ignored local government completely, and except for fairly large numbers of young teachers the councils were quickly dominated by men of little education or ability, and even less integrity. Accordingly the following years brought succeeding scandals of irresponsibility, in which crude politics and crude corruption were intermingled, and which resulted—even before the military *coups* and the Nigerian civil war brought normal administration to a halt—in virtually every council in southern Nigeria and Sierra Leone being dissolved, while those in Ghana had become mere appendages of the CPP. There is no point in elaborating the details of this story—they are sufficiently well known. The point that perhaps needs emphasis is that the chance of responsible local government was offered but was thrown away, and that it will be a long time before any responsible West African Government is likely to take a similar chance. Hence the compromises that they are currently seeking.

Yet the local authorities might have survived the corruption of the councillors—since corruption and inefficiency do not necessarily go hand in hand, and indeed some say that corruption is a spur to action—if they had not from the start been so seriously handicapped by a shortage of resources and trained staff. It has been a constant theme of this book that it is self-evident that if a country is underdeveloped, money, equipment and skill must be scarce, and that one of the main tasks of Government is to deploy what there is to the best advantage. To dissipate them, as was done in Ghana and southern Nigeria, between the original field organization of Government and the new local authorities has been to spread them too thinly, and in practice has left local government with no staff to speak of outside the office. The position was made worse by the petty local politics which caused the fragmentation of the larger councils, the only ones which had a chance to be effective.

To sum up so far, a system of local government was devised in the first place to satisfy political aspirations; an attempt was then made to staff it. The alternative method would have been to make an inventory of resources and then to have seen how best they could be administratively channelled. Perhaps the greatest gain of the last ten years is that heads are now cool enough to consider this second approach on its merits, for almost everything that is being done today is in direct reaction against specific failures of the 1950–1970 era. These trends, which we have noticed throughout the book, we must now try to summarize.

From local government to local administration

First, there is the very obvious tendency, which we have noted throughout the earlier part of this book, to continue the firm grip which central governments resumed over local authorities during the 'twilight' years of roughly 1966–71.

It is perhaps most explicitly stated in the Local Administration Law in Ghana, where central control has a political as well as an administrative meaning. Even at the level of the district—the genuine local unit—the chairman is appointed by the Prime Minister and the officers are civil servants and not local government employees. In the Western and Mid-West States of Nigeria local government staff retain their separate identity (though now on a basis of equality with the civil service), but the DO, at divisional level, is given effective control, and in the Eastern States the new forms of local administration are in their very different ways projections of the central authority. In Sierra Leone it seems certain as we write that the district and chiefdom councils will again be subjected to the direct oversight of that versatile man, the District Officer of

Government. In the Northern States of Nigeria the age-old independence of the NAs to employ their own staff has been modified in five states out of six, and local government staffs have been 'unified' in varying degrees, in addition to which the traditional power of the district heads is being eroded in two States at least by the DO's authority over the new 'administrative areas'.

The general pattern is thus consistent throughout West Africa, and is a natural consequence of the failures which we discussed earlier. On the whole its justice is recognized and there is little disposition to resist the revival of central administrative authority; there is however (in Ghana) an under-current of feeling against the *politicisation* of the post of district chairman, even among those who are prepared to accept a political chairman and a civil service secretary at the regional level. The region, it is felt, is concerned with large-scale strategic planning and is the rightful instrument of the Government, but the district is concerned with local affairs and is the rightful instrument of the people.

The DO or DC[2] remained a key figure in the administration of government after independence, but his position in relation to the local authorities became uncertain, and he lacked the unquestioned all-round authority of his expatriate predecessor. Recent events have again put him in effective charge of local administration, but his position is not an easy one. His predecessor had certain advantages which are gone forever. In the colonial régime he ranked superior to the local departmental heads; he was moreover a magistrate, which gave him great prestige among the local people; finally the mere fact of being the white representative of the colonial power made his actions largely unchallengable, even if he was often young and his

[2] One of the minor confusions has always been that the District Officer in Ghana was called a District Commissioner. Perhaps the best description was achieved at one stage by the Government of Ghana when they abolished the title and replaced it with the straightforward one of Government Agent.

actions sometimes foolish. His African successor is generally even younger, but lacks these fortuitous advantages, and he does not have the same inherited authority over departmental colleagues, who not infrequently go over his head to the directors of their own departments. He tends to become in practice the local head of one particular department, i.e. local government, by whatever name it may be known.

There is no insoluble problem here, but it is a new relationship, the future of which has yet to be hammered out in experience, and meanwhile the human factor is of great importance.

Restriction of the rôle of councillors

The other unmistakable trend is to restrict the future activities of elected councillors, who on the whole disgraced themselves in the first local government era of 1950–70. There are of course few elected councillors in West Africa at the time of writing, except (since 1971) in Ghana. There will presumably be none in Nigeria (outside the City of Lagos) until the end of military rule, though as a stop-gap there are the various kinds of nominated committees that we have described. In Sierra Leone the same position will apply until the Government makes up its mind about the future of local administration in general.

There have been more than enough inquests on the corruption and inefficiency of elected councillors in the past, and there is no point in adding here to what everybody knows. On the other hand it is sufficiently clear from laws, edicts and policy statements that it is the intention ultimately to revert to local elections, and we can begin to see the way the wind is blowing so far as the councillor's future rôle is concerned.

In the first place the principle of indirect election, which was once anathema, is again finding some favour. We discussed its pros and cons as an instrument of representative government on page 85 and all that it is necessary to add here is that among the reasons for a willingness to revive it are its cheapness and simplicity compared with direct elections, and the fact that it is less likely to turn local authorities into party political battlefields.

More to the immediate point is the growing popularity of the single 'executive', or 'standing' or 'policy' committee to replace the spectrum of committees copied from English local government. The supposed advantages of spreading responsibility were purely theoretical and it was in these committees that councillors both interfered in day-to-day administration and practised corruption over contracts. What is now desired is that councillors should be restricted to discussing policy, leaving everything else to their staffs. The popular way of putting this is that 'the deliberative and executive functions should be divorced'. In its highest terms this means that councillors should decide priorities; in its lowest terms it means that they should not be allowed to interfere in administration, especially in appointments and contracts.

The complement of the single executive committee is a single Executive Officer with wider powers than the English type of *primus inter pares* Clerk.[3] West African local authorities are as yet too small, and too restricted in their activities, to talk sensibly in terms of modern managerial techniques, but the management *idea* has become more attractive than democratic control, given that democratic control means party politics, corruption and nepotism.

This leads us, however, to the point that elected councillors have returned in Ghana and may be expected to return in due course in Nigeria and Sierra Leone, which raises the question whether we may expect better things from them in future than in the past. The restriction of their rôle will limit their opportunities for doing harm, but why should we have elected councillors at all if we are forced to consider the question in this negative way?

[3] In fact, this idea has virtually disappeared in England; for several years the title has been 'Clerk and Chief Executive Officer', and managerial rather than legal qualifications are sought.

Why should those elected at the next round of local elections be any better than their predecessors? Why indeed did those elected the first time round contain so many rogues and self-seekers, and why did the professional and commercial middle classes stand aside from local government?

It will be impossible to solve the problem unless governments are prepared to show moral courage and to take certain unpopular steps. Anyone who as a councillor has been involved in bribery and corruption in the past ought surely to be disqualified from standing again, and the qualifications for a candidate could well be higher than those of a voter—in age, education, standing in the community, or some combination of these. If governments are so irresolute that steps of this kind are beyond them it would clearly be better to have a permanently centralized form of administration, and to have done with representative local government altogether. Equally, if educated and responsible people are not interested in democracy to the extent of seeking to be councillors we cannot hope to improve on direct central administration.

The rôle of Chiefs

Before leaving the subject of councillors we must recall that another very general trend at the moment is to restore to the chiefs the minority of seats that they occupied on local councils in the 1950s. This is not necessarily to commend the idea, which has much to be said against it. Chiefs cannot retain their natural or traditional authority if they can be outvoted or defeated in argument by elected commoners; alternatively if a chief's prestige is properly honoured those who disagree with him cannot speak freely in council in his presence.

The problem of the chiefs is that the decline in authority which they share with royalty and aristocracy the world over has not yet penetrated very far below the surface of African society. If they are to be left out of modern local government arrangements because they are an anachronism, how does one take into account the fact that they are still the most effective means of communication in those matters with which local government is primarily concerned?

The question is unanswerable, or rather its answer lies in the passage of time. It must work itself out, as it has had to do in earlier civilizations, with the gradual evolution of society. We do not know whether, generations hence, African societies will have done away with chieftainship; whether they will retain the tradition and ceremony but divorce it from practical affairs; or whether chieftaincy will remain an integral part of government. We are at an awkward transitional time when the educated minority are divided in their view and the uneducated majority accept the older tradition. It will not be possible to form a settled view until the educated minority becomes the educated majority.

Local Autonomy and Central Control

We have implied that West Africa has now crossed the line which divides local government from local administration. In fact there is no such line, or if there is it is invisible, for local government can tolerate a good deal of central control and still remain self-respecting and representative. It is however true that some basic essentials of local government are being endangered by the new arrangements or plans that we have described.

For example, local government must surely imply diffusion of power within the state, whereas power in West Africa is becoming steadily more centralized; it must imply local leadership which is locally accountable, and this is impossible if chairmen are to be appointed by the central government for political reasons; some think that it must also imply that local authorities employ their own staff, whereas in parts of West Africa the public service has replaced the local government service, or the two are indistinguishable. The change in the title of this book from *'Local Government'* to *'Local Administration'* in *West Africa* seems therefore to be justified.

On the other hand these changes are not universal throughout West Africa, and in Nigeria the situation will to some extent be fluid until the end of military rule, when elected councils will change the face of local government yet again.

It is therefore worth reflecting that the English type of local autonomy, which has inevitably been taken as a yardstick, is not essential for a self-respecting system of local government. Admittedly some systems, for example the Scandinavian and West German, have even more autonomy; on the other hand many systems throughout the world have a great deal less. In the context of this book a digression into *Irish* local government is justified, partly because it offers a reasonable compromise between local autonomy and central control, and partly because there are some interesting historical parallels between Ireland and West Africa in their relation to the United Kingdom.

Local Government in the Irish Republic[4]

Ireland was governed as part of the United Kingdom until 1922, with the full apparatus of British central and local government controlled from Whitehall. In 1922 it became a 'Free State' within the British Commonwealth, in the manner of a dominion; in 1937 it became an independent country in the manner later followed by Ghana, i.e. with a presidential form of government, linked to the Commonwealth only through recognition of the Monarch as head of the 'family'; in 1949 it left the Commonwealth as an independent Republic. These developments had their consequences for local government.

From 1922 onwards the British form of local government suffered a decline. Inefficiency was rife, partly because of war-time neglect but partly because councillors were elected

---

[4] I am indebted to Mr Hubert Allen for assistance with this section. His dissertation 'Under New Management' is based on careful research in the Irish Republic in 1968/69. Library of the Institute of Local Government Studies, University of Birmingham.

to promote the cause of nationalism rather than of sound administration, which caused ratepayers to revolt and Government to withhold grants. There was also a certain amount of corruption, which was exploited by the Government beyond its real deserts in order to discredit political opponents. But the more fundamental fact was that the system was unsuitable for Ireland. The British system had evolved in a wealthy country and at a time when revenues were buoyant, for it is not a cheap form of government; Ireland by contrast was a poor country. Britain was industrial and urban, but with a prosperous rural population of middle-class country dwellers and large-scale farmers; Ireland was predominantly a country of small—indeed to a large extent peasant subsistence—farmers. Britain could therefore draw on a considerable class of prosperous people who were public spirited and to whom local government was a hobby; Ireland could not. Communications in Britain were good, so that councillors could travel easily and quickly to their innumerable committee meetings; this was not so in Ireland.

Accordingly, independent Ireland set about devising its own system of local government based on county and city 'managers', which took shape as early as 1928 and was consolidated in the County Management Acts of 1940 and 1942. This system was essentially a compromise between a number of other systems, and a student of comparative local government could find in it elements of British, German and American origin. The essential fact is that it suited the circumstances of Ireland. What emerged from these Acts was a difference of emphasis between the respective responsibilities of the manager and the council, as compared with those of the English clerk and council. The method of appointing the manager was significant, for this was not left to the free choice of the council; the manager was appointed by them on the recommendation of the 'Local Appointments Commissioners' (a kind of Local Government Service Board), who would normally recommend, if they were candidates, an existing county secretary or secretary to a board of health; thus the appointment was ministerially controlled. The manager, once appointed, assumed a much larger degree of executive responsibility than his British counterpart, though not as much as his counterpart—the city manager—in many American cities, whose rôle is closer to that of the managing director of a business firm *vis-à-vis* his board of directors.

This did not, however, mean that the function of the elected councils was ornamental, or that their powers were negligible. On the contrary all the *essential* powers of democratic local government were specifically reserved to them in a Schedule of the 1940 Act; they included, notably, the power to make a rate, to borrow money, to make, amend or revoke a by-law, to award scholarships, and to make certain decisions under the Town and Regional Planning and the Housing Acts. What it did mean, however, in practice, was that the county councils confined themselves to decisions of policy on these major matters, but did not hold such frequent meetings, nor break up into such an elaborate network of committees, as their British counterparts, for the purpose of supervising in detail the way in which policy was implemented. This was not necessarily less democratic than British practice, which indeed involves some very curious paradoxes, since some committees and sub-committees are apt to lose themselves in discussion of very minor details which should be decided by officials, while leaving officials a remarkable amount of freedom in major matters of policy; or again they will haggle over the expenditure of a few pounds on some item which happens to have caught their attention, and then pass the expenditure of hundreds of thousands without a second thought. The Irish county councils had of course full supervisory powers and in an extremity they could, by a two-thirds majority, suspend a manager and, with the Minister's consent, remove him; there was thus no doubt that the council was the controlling power. The difference of emphasis lay in the way in which local government is tackled as a problem in *management*.

These arrangements were amended by the Local Government (County Administration) Act of 1955, which again altered the balance of authority between the professional administrator and the elected representative. For example, councils were empowered by resolution to require the manager to do *any* lawful act, even one which was reserved to him by previous legislation as an 'executive function'. But although this represented a 'swing of the pendulum' back towards British ideas, the diffusion of responsibility was still less than in Britain and the independence of the chief officer greater. As to council committees, they hardly exist outside the City of Dublin to this day.

Most significantly, the manager system saw Ireland through the first generation of independence, when the withdrawal of British controlled officials had left the local authorities in an awkward stage of transition. The similarities between the historical development of local government in Ireland and West Africa are too striking to need emphasis, and although it is perhaps tempting to push these further than is warranted,[5] the experience of Ireland is likely to be more relevant to that of West Africa than that of Britain, and it is certainly the view of West African governments today that local government has in the past involved too many councillors, too many committees and too much interference in the realm of management.

Here, then, is one possible development in the future of control. There are many others. At the opposite extreme, for example, there is control by the 'executive councillors' in the Northern States of Nigeria, which we have already discussed. What is necessary above all is to preserve an open mind, to refuse to be influenced by the practice of other countries where circumstances are wholly different, and to settle on a system of control which will, in *local* circumstances, satisfy as far as possible two needs which are always apt to be in conflict with one another—representative control on the one hand and managerial efficiency

[5] Hubert Allen, *op. cit.*, discusses in some detail how far the comparison is actually valid.

on the other. It is one of the dilemmas of democracy that the two do not always coincide, and that a compromise has to be devised between them.

Areas and Functions

After this digression, there is a final trend to be recorded in West Africa, in which a number of apparently disconnected things are happening, but which are part of underlying changes in area and function, a matter which we discussed on page 50.

One aspect of this is seen in southern Nigeria and Ghana, where, as we have several times suggested, one cause of the progressive weakness of local government has been that of the original three-tier system the top and bottom tiers tended to disappear, leaving a medium-sized area that was too small to provide effective results but too large to draw upon local loyalties. We can see with hindsight that it might have been better to have left the upper tier, which, though impersonal, might have commanded the resources to get results; and the lowest tier which, though too small to do much in its own name, could command village patriotism. The Ghanaian and Nigerian State Governments are on the whole now tending to this view. As a typical example the Western State Government is proposing 51 new divisional authorities in place of the existing 114, thus going 'upwards', but supplementing them with area committees at the grass-roots, thus going 'downwards'.

The new trend is in response to the demand that all local government activity should be directed towards 'development', for which the medium-sized authority is ill-equipped. Big authorities can command resources, small authorities can engage interest, but medium-sized authorities can do neither. It is open to question whether the Western State solution, for example, is sufficiently radical to satisfy the first criterion. As to the second, it is interesting that over the whole of southern Nigeria and Ghana the term 'community development' is now being appropriated to define the function of the small councils. For many years it has meant everything and nothing. In Ghana it has created a large government department; in Nigeria it has meant very little; in academic circles it has been propounded as a philosophy and a way of life.

A very different aspect of the same process of adapting area to function may be seen in some parts (though not in all) of the Northern States, where for example the Emirates of Kano and Katsina, formerly co-terminous with really powerful Native Authorities, are now, under their new name of Local Government Authorities, to be subdivided into administrative areas in order to 'bring government nearer to the people'. Although the resources of these areas may well be as great as those of the new divisions of the Western State they nevertheless represent a move away from the really large authority which other States might envy, and towards the medium-sized authority which they have come to regret. No doubt political reasons were a determining factor, but it is noteworthy that while the Northern States are equally anxious that all local administration should be geared to development they argue that smaller units are needed (e.g. smaller than the Kano Local Government Authority), whereas Ghana and the rest of Nigeria argue the opposite.

'Development'

Throughout West Africa it is now said in speeches and policy documents that whereas native administration in colonial days, and local government in the 1950s and 1960s, was designed only to ensure law and order, local government in the future is to be designed to promote development. In fact, a comparison of the amounts spent on schools, clinics, roads, water supplies, agriculture and so on, on the one hand, and the NA police and prisons on the other, shows that this has never been true since records were kept. The point is worth mentioning because although 'Local Government for Development' is an attractive slogan there may be some disillusionment if its results prove to be much as they have always been, or even if they are improvements but of the same general order. In the Northern States in particular the Native Authorities have been responsible for considerable developments since the beginning of the century, and the development expediture of authorities elsewhere, however modest, has consistently risen and never fallen.

The narrowing scope of local government

It must, however, be noted that during the 1950–70 era local government (or native administrative where it continued to be so-called) was getting narrower in its scope. From the outset of this era the wide powers given to local authorities on paper tended to mean little, not only because they lacked the ability to exercise them but because provincial and regional heads of departments resisted the incursion of local government into what had always been a central government field. They were not prepared to see their professional work mishandled by inexperienced councils, who were mainly interested in politics and perquisites, and it cannot be said that Governments made any attempt to come to the local authorities' rescue. On the contrary, they started to by-pass local government themselves. Town planning, for example, was a local government function in all the early legislation, but when governments discovered how much expertise was required they created their own agencies. Agriculture and natural resources—basic to development—have also largely passed from local to central control, though this has been because the local authorities themselves displayed little interest in them. More surprisingly primary education, though not centrally controlled, is tending to become the responsibility of special authorities rather than the multi-purpose local authorities. In Nigeria, for example, local education authorities are *ad hoc* bodies, differently constituted and differently financed from the ordinary local authorities.

This general tendency is of course encouraged in Nigeria by the mere fact of division into States. Although the

Northern States vary very greatly in size there are undeniably six State Governments in place of one Regional Government, and certain services are administered on a State-wide basis, whereas a region-wide basis would have been impossible. The Kano Local Government Authority, for example, has lost control of urban water supplies, a printing press and even a number of markets. Indeed, the State provides a vivid example of the problem of area and function, for if the State is small enough the need for large-scale local government must clearly diminish. To take this to its logical conclusion, if the political state is a small island, as happens in various parts of the world, there is no need for local government at all.

Such considerations as these bring us full circle to the third chapter of the book, in which we discussed the principles governing the question of 'who should do what?'. They also strike a responsive chord in any English writer, since the English have been living for some years in the expectation of local government reforms, and reform of a radical kind is now approaching the statute book. The core of the English problem has been that the actual structure of local authorities has remained unchanged since the late nineteenth century, when the system was first devised. It served its purpose well for twenty-five years; for the next twenty-five it showed signs of strain; for the last twenty-five the strain has become serious, for during these seventy-five years every other aspect of life has changed, sometimes almost beyond recognition. The system has continued to work, and indeed to provide social services and public works on a massive scale, but at the cost of a good deal of duplication and waste. There are too many small authorities; there is a division between town and country which was valid when it was made but is no longer so; and even the major local authorities cannot measure up in size to the probable demands of the next half century. Accordingly the number of local authorities is to be reduced, by amalgamating urban and rural authorities and, also whole counties, to a quarter of the present number, following the two-year investigation and research of the Royal Commission on Local Government, widely known as the Redcliffe-Maud Commission.

It is unprofitable to compare the details of local government in Britain with those in West Africa, but the Redcliffe-Maud Commission illustrates a universal principle, namely that local government areas must keep in step with changing technology. If they fail to do so their efficiency will diminish and it is likely that public boards or government departments will gradually whittle away their functions, leaving them with lesser tasks appropriate to their size and resources. The only exceptional thing about the British situation has been that successive British Governments have been slow to impose change, and since they were under no compulsion to do so, and since the opposition to change was formidable, matters were allowed to drift. One can perhaps draw a moral from this and say that an important feature of any new local government legislation —in West Africa or elsewhere—ought to be a statutory obligation to review the system not less than every ten years.

This book has been an attempt to examine an activity which absorbed an extraordinarily high proportion of the energies of West African governments between 1950 and 1970, which has some value as a case study in comparative administration, which has had many failures and disappointments, but which has on the other hand been an unavoidable necessity. For although there has been no lack of criticism of what has been done, no critics have maintained that what preceded it was better, or have been able to say with confidence how the transition from a local tribal parliament to a modern-type local authority could have been more adroitly guided, given not only the undoubted need but the irresistible demand for the latter.

The transformation began, in 1950, in the Eastern Region of Nigeria. It would be ironic, though perhaps appropriate, to end this account where it began, in that same part of

Nigeria. For the new South Eastern State has abolished local government in disgust and the East Central State now believes that salvation lies in grafting modern bureaucratic forms on to the traditional lineage and age-groups. But Ghana and Nigeria, who followed close behind the Eastern Region of Nigeria in 1951 and 1952, are persisting in principle with what they first created, though coming near to replacing local government by local administration.

INDEX

administrative officers (colonial), 14
Alderfer, Harold F., 17, 19, 20, 28
audit, 72, 73

British colonial administration, 13, 14
by-laws, 58, 59

Chiefs, 152–8, 223, 224
cities of West Africa compared, 139–51
committee system, 88, 89
contracts, 60
conventions, 89
councillors:
  general, 76–94
  duties of, 86–8
  election of, 85, 86
  relationship to staff, 103–5
  remuneration of, 79–81
  restriction of rôle, 221–3
courts, local, 14, 155

decentralization and devolution, 13–26, 34, 49; restraints on devolution, 44, 45
default powers, 68
delegated authority to local rulers, 31
delegated legislation, 69
District Councils (Sierra Leone), 158–62, 163–5

education, 29, 41–3, 51, 52
elections, 47

family planning, 48
fees for services, 132, 133
Freetown, 147, 148

Ghana, local government in, 166–78
Gold Coast, 145–7
grants, 119–24

Ibadan, 143, 144
inspection, 73

Joint Bodies (Joint Boards and Committees), 63–5

Kaduna, 144
Kano, 145

Lagos, 140–3
law and order, 57, 58
licences, 133, 134
loans, 134, 135
local authorities:
  and education, 41–3
  as agents of Government, 49, 67, 70
  constitutional duties, 54–60
  duties and powers, 55, 56
  relationship with central government, 41–53, 66–75
  relationship with each other, 60–6
  revenue, 119–35
  size and structure, 50, 54–75, 98–109; British, 95–8
  trade unions, 108, 109
local government:
  and economics, 37–9
  and geography, 31–4
  and history, 27–31
  and politics, 36, 37
  and sociology, 34–6
  in Eire, 225–9
  other systems of, 17–24, 27–31

Minister, powers of, 72

'Natural rulers' of West Africa, 30, 31, 34
Nigeria, local government in, 179–215; Eastern Region, 180–90; Western Region, 190–8; Northern Region, 198–215

party politics, 104, 105, 110–18; Sardauna of Sokoto, statement by, 115–17
politics and local government, 36, 37
precepts, 157

rates, 124–32
religion, 35

Sardauna of Sokoto, statement by, 115–17

Sierra Leone, local government in, 151–65
'sons of the soil', 99
staffs of local authorities, 23–4
  relationship to central government, 98–102
  relationship to councillors, 103–5
subordinate authorities, 65, 66

tax, 124–32
'tiers', 60–3
townships (Sierra Leone), 162, 163
trade unions in local government, 108, 109
traditional members, 91–4

ultra vires, 56, 57